W9-BNL-162

The Legacy of Kanakuk

By Darnell White

Timothy Publishing
1353 Lake Shore Drive
Branson MO 65616-9470

Manufactured in the United States of America

Library of Congress Control Number: 2008905504

ISBN: 978-0-9818902-0-3

"THANKS FOR THE MEMORIES"

A year or so after Spike died I had a nudge to tell some of the stories of Kanakuk Kamps starting from the beginning in 1926. As I was the only one who knew the early years' history, I felt that I owed it to Spike and Coach Lantz to document the dates and history that I heard from them. I sincerely hope that you will enjoy the stories and the priceless pictures that "are better than a thousand words." Many stories were passed on to me by erstwhile Kampers and staff who have stayed "in touch" with Kanakuk. Many have generously sent pictures from their Kamp scrapbooks. Thank you for sharing and reminiscing on "how we were."

It has been fulfilling to share and work with Jamie Jo White Braner, our first grand-daughter, who has done a remarkable presentation with the pictures and layout. Jamie Jo is now writing "the rest of the story" about Kanakuk Kamps from where I left off until the present. For me, working along-side Jamie Jo, has added the "punch" the stories needed to ensure a better presentation in book form. Thank you, Jamie Jo.

Spike's and my three sons, Bob, Bill, and Joe and their precious wives have encouraged me in the writings. Bob and Bill have called me from Texas often with details of stories. If you knew Bill, you would be grinning, knowing that Bill's suggestions would give the best laughs, but not the best choice of memorabilia. Our grandchildren have given me many needed "pats-on-the-back" via phone calls and e-mails. With Joe's and Debbie Jo's good neighborly boost, this "back-to-the-future" has been a sentimental trip. Thank you, Family.

Chris Stange, Kanakuk's Senior Director of Finance, and my co-horts in the Accounting Department have given helpful understanding as I have written most of the stories here in my office on "Company time." Tena Terrell was helpful, teaching computer skills for the efficiency and organization of the stories. Thank you for your participation.

Special thanks and gratitude go to Spike for his dedication, dreams, and devotion to Kanakuk Kamps, and especially for the lifestyle, worthy training and experiences for our sons during their "up-bringing" and to their families, and to me.

Finally, a rounding "Standing 'O'" to GOD who protected and guided Coach Lantz, Spike, Joe and Debbie Jo, the Staff, the Kampers and their parents down through the generations.

"And GOD said, 'Well done'"

Darnell White

KANAKUK-KANAKOMO KAMPS LAKESHORE DRIVE BRANSON, MISSOURI 65616

"PATCHES OF THE PAST"
LET THE FUTURE KNOW OF THE PAST

When Kanakuk's Administration Building was constructed and all Departments and Warehouse were "settled in," Don Frank, KUK's CFO and I were standing in the reception area of the third floor, and Don remarked, "The walls are bare and need pictures," (just exactly my thought!) and without hesitating, asked, "How about old pictures and memorabilia of Kanakuk Kamp as far back as 1926?" I was soaring at the prospects of delving deeply into saved boxes of preserved catalogs, records, family cards, ribbons, awards, and pictures which would "speak more than a thousand words!" Today, these walls hold revived treasures and they are displayed throughout the building.

Kamp staff 1931 Top row left, Lucile White, Spike's mother.

Since Spike's demise, Jamie Jo and I have harbored the desire to document the story of Kanakuk in book form. It's not unusual for erstwhile Kampers, staff members, and families - now third, fourth, and fifth generations* involved with Kanakuk Kamps - to drop by my office to visit and talk about "the good old days at Kanakuk." From days of yore to present time, they all seem to revel in looking at and reminiscing over the pictures on these walls. They are sentimental about their memories. Many tell me they walk around Kamp to visit their Tribal Campfire Meeting place and look in their cabins to see if their names are still where they wrote them on walls and rafters (if they can't find their names, they get a marker and see that it is!)

Perhaps this book will stir up memories for you. You are a part of the Kanakuk Family!

*Spike's MOM was Head Cook in 1931. Spike was on staff and his brother Jo-Jo was a Kamper. My mother, Pardner, "Kanakuk's Flower Lady," planted and nourished the flowers all over Kanakuk until she was 92 years of age. Hays Braner, the first great-great-grandson, has attended Kanakuk since 2004, and Ashlynn Hays White, great granddaughter, started as a Kamper in 2005, making the White family a Fifth Generation Family. And there are several more soon to join their siblings and/or cousins.

Above middle of row: JoJo White, Spikes brother. Below: Spike and Darnell with their honor Kamper grandsons, Scott and Lance

Above: Spike and Darnell. Right: Pardner, Darnell's mother, with her great grandkids: Lance, Scott, Jamie Jo, Wesley and Cody.

"IN THE BEGINNING . . . "

Mr. C. L. Ford began Kuggaho Camp for Boys in 1926. Coach Ed Walker from Dallas, Texas (the father of the famous Doak Walker) and Coach Bill Lantz from Tulsa were on the staff of Mr. Ford's Kuggaho Kamp.

In the spring of 1931, Spike was hired by Mr. Ford because he liked the sports Spike played at Amarillo High School. He played Varsity Tennis and Basketball (later Spike played on the Varsity Basketball Team at Texas A&M), had his American Red Cross Certificate for Swimming, Life Saving and Life Guarding, and was an Eagle Scout. Spike had also spent a lot of time learning Indian lore and dancing with the Indians in Taos, New Mexico.

Spike's mother, Mary Lucile Ross White, had a Master's degree in Diet and Nutrition, and Mr. Ford offered her the job of Head Cook at Kuggaho. She accepted the offer because she was reluctant for both boys (Spike and his younger brother "Jo Jo") to travel so far away and spend all summer at a camp in Missouri that she knew little about. Spike's dad drove the family to Branson and returned home when Kuggaho closed for the summer.

After 1932, Mr. Ford left Camp Kuggaho and Coach Lantz purchased and continued to run the boys' camp under a new name, Kanakuk Kamp. Many years later, Mr. Ford started a girls' camp, Camp Kickapoo in Kerrville, Texas. Kickapoo continues to be a reputable and popular camp, being operated by Mr. Ford's family. His grandsons were Kampers at Kanakuk when Spike had Kanakuk Kamp.

During the years 1926-1934, Mr. Ford also ran a Girls' Camp, Kickapoo Camp, across the Lake from Kanakuk on Bee Creek. "Lady Bee" O'Brien, mother of **Davey O'Brien, was the Staff Director. When Spike was a Kanakuk counselor, he dated one of the counselors. (Uncle Bill let Spike use a canoe from Kanakuk Kamp to paddle to Bee Creek for his "date." I think they just paddled around the Lake and got acquainted?) Years later, after Spike and I met and married and lived in College Station, I met the counselor, Louise Oliver, and we became friends.

Forty years later, Spike and Joe invited members of C.A.M.P., mostly camps at Kerrville in the Hill Country, to get together in Missouri after the summer session closed. A large group from Texas joined Kanakuk in bonding. Two of the women had attended Mr. Ford's camp for Girls on Bee Creek, and Spike offered them the opportunity to "go back in time." They canoed to the campsite and found concrete stones where the stage had been when they were campers. They jumped on the location of the stage, danced, put on a skit, and became "kids" again. Spike was the sole spectator. He loved having had that rare and delightful experience.

*Doak Walker played in a play pen outside the same location of Kanakuk office today. Little did anyone know how famous this toddler would become in the Sports World.

**Davey O'Brien was a Kanakuk Kamper for several years, and Coach Lantz, from the start, liked his athletic prowess. Though he was small in stature, he was BIG in heart, discipline and dedication.

CARLETON'S SWIMMERS, KUGGAHO CAMP 1932

REDCROSS LIFE SAVERS, KUGGAHO CAMP, 1932

CAMP FLEET KUGGAHO KAMP 1931

TRAVELING TO KUGGAHO

--Summer 1932--

With Spike at the wheel and Jo Jo as co-pilot, their dog, JoCar rode in the back. (Jo for Spike's brother, and Car for Carlton, Spike's name). The jazzy automobile Spike bought for a mere $10.00. The following fall, Spike drove the car from Amarillo to Texas A & M. Since cadets were not allowed to have cars, the Ford was stored and hidden under a haystack at a family farm in Midway (halfway between Bryan and College Station, TX) until Christmas break.

"Where did the name Kanakuk come from?"

The name Kanakuk comes from the Kickapoo Indian tribe. The Kickapoo were violent Indians and Kanakuk was a prophet who embraced pacifism. A great deal of his religion concerned methods of tribal self-improvement here on earth. He advocated agriculture as the mainstay of Kickapoo economic life, instead of practice of pursuing game in far-off hunting grounds. Most importantly, he preached absolute abstinence from alcohol and the rewards that would come to those who worked hard.

Kanakuk means "the loved one." The name surely has had its imprint and happy memories to our "loved ones" and to scores of other Kanakukers and their families, as well.

In Honor of Davey O'Brien

The Outstanding All-American Football Player of 1938

Many critics have rated Davey O'Brien as one of the greatest football players of all time. Most of the sports fans who have seen him on the football field have picked him as their favorite. There is no doubt that Davey is one of the "Greats" field general, forward passer, field goal passer, as a field goal kicker, and as an all-around player. But to those of us who have known him intimately, he is at the very top as a sportsman, a gentleman and an all-around fellow.

Davey attended his first summer at Kanakuk when he was ten, and attended each of the following six summers. As a little fellow, Davey was always a hustler and a fighter. He played to win, but always gave his team mates credit for winning, and took the blame on himself when they lost. He never offered an alibi, and always congratulated an opponent who had defeated him.

Davey trained and worked hard during his summers at Kamp and during his last year was given the camp award as the "Best All-Around Kamper." While Davey received many of the country's outstanding trophies in 1938, he said the camp award meant more to him than any other because if he hadn't won the camp award, he wouldn't have learned the lessons of life that made it possible to win the others.

Here's to Davey O'Brien, the " All-American Boy," an old Kanakuk Kamper, as quarterback on the all-star team which is a great honor for a freshman in the professional league. Davey established a great record his first season in pro ball, breaking all existing forward pass records in the league; number of passes completed in one game, number of passes completed in a season, and the number of yards gained by completed passes in a season.

This year, Davey was again an outstanding player in the professional league, and broke a couple of his previous records. Now Davey sets another example for American youth. Davey turned down one of the best offers ever made to a professional football player to become a special agent in the F.B.I. (G-Man). He feels that in a time like this it is his duty to serve his country.

So our "All-American Boy" goes on to new glory to uphold the ideal of true American youth.

FOOTBALL HALL OF FAME

Souvenir Suppleme

ROBERT DAVID O'BRIEN

FROGS' O'BRIEN JOINS RANK OF GRID IMMORTALS

At halftime of today's traditional game between TCU and SMU, one of the Frogs' all-time greats will be formally inducted into the National Football Foundation's Hall of Fame. With fitting ceremony, Robert David O'Brien will be presented with the plaque that places him among the game's immortals.

In 1938, the 150-pound Dallas boy wrote many bright new pages of football history as he led the TCU team to 11 straight victories including the Sugar Bowl and No. 1 ranking in the nation.

Standing only 5 feet, 7 inches tall but powerfully built, the rugged little man caught the imagination of the country as he passed, ran and sparked the 1938 team to victory after victory.

At season's end, he was a choice for All-American maki tions. He was also voted the fa Trophy as the outstanding am of the year, and received it i in New York City.

This year 21 former coache were elected to the Hall of F the total number to 127. Sa TCU's other member. Matty Frog coach and now athlet SMU, was also elected this y

Although he played every seasons, O'Brien never took t injury. Newspaper dubbed h Knot."

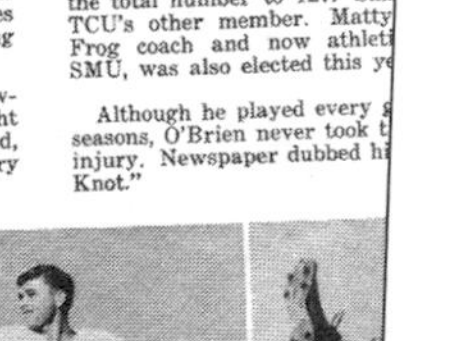

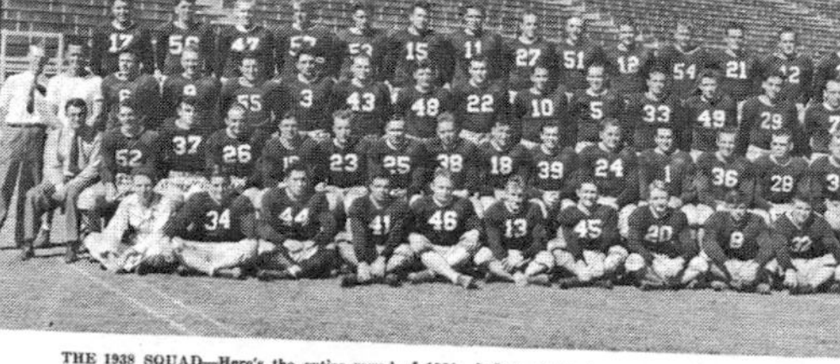

THE 1938 SQUAD—Here's the entire squad of 1938. Left to right, front row: Palmer (manager), Allen, Sherrod, Shook, Binion, Best, Taylor, Cowart, O'Brien, Short, Mosley (manager).
Second row: Grubbs (athletic director), Cobb, Malone, Smith, Pratt, McClanahan, Horner, Taylor, White, Duckworth, Kline, Chamberlain, Clark, Hampton, Kerlee, Clark (assistant coach).
Third row: Smith (trainer), Roach (freshman coach), Ware, Kellow, Stanley, Anderson, Cook, Co-Capt. Aldrich, Capt. Hale, Hall, Clifford, Wilkinson, Alexander, Pugh, Herring, Brumbelow (line coach), Meyer (head coach).
Fourth row: Ehlers, Childers, Snow, Loos, Lowe, McWhorter, Hensch, Jordan, Sparks, Odle, Smith, Williams, Perryman, Looney.

DAVEY'S RECORD OUTSTANDING

David O'Brien was one of the finest all-around players in the history of the Southwest Conference. He was a good runner and punter, an outstanding selector of plays and certainly one of the three or four top passers in the area's history.

As a sophomore in 1936, he played behind the great Sammy Baugh who was a senior. That year he fired only 40 passes but hit 21 for a .526 average. In 1937 as a junior, he took over full responsibility for the Frog offense and after a shaky start, the team won its last three Conference games handily.

Then came 1938 and TCU's greatest season. That year, O'Brien shattered records right and left as he passed 194 times, completed 110 for 1733 yards and had only 4 tosses intercepted. The 110 completions are still high for the Conference although tied by Baylor's Burke in 1949 and SMU's Benners in 1951.

The 1733 yards passing is still the all-time Conference record. Burke's 1428 paces is second.

Davey's record for three full years on the varsity was:

Year	Pas. At.	Com.	Inc.	Int.	Yards	Pct.
1936	40	21	15	4	252	.526
1937	237	96	122	19	947	.405
1938	194	110	80	4	1733	.567
Totals	471	227	217	27	2932	.482

As a reward for his great season, O'Brien made almost every all-American team that was picked.

The list included: Associated Press, United Press, the Grantland Rice team, Collyer's Eye, New York Sun, Eddie Dooley, Kate Smith, International News Service, Life Magazine, All-American Board, N.E.A., Williamson Ratings, Liberty Magazine.

Since most of them presented watches, Davey had more time-pieces than he could wear or carry.

Later in professional ball he set a record for number of passes completed in one game. He served with the FBI for several years and is now associated with an oil firm in Fort Worth. He married his TCU sweetheart, Frances Buster, and they have a growing family.

DAVEY'S TROPHY—Here's the Heisman Trophy that was presented to David O'Brien by the New York Downtown Club at the end of the 1938 season. The Frog ace was voted the outstanding amateur athlete in the nation.

"Pardon me boy, is that the Kanakuk

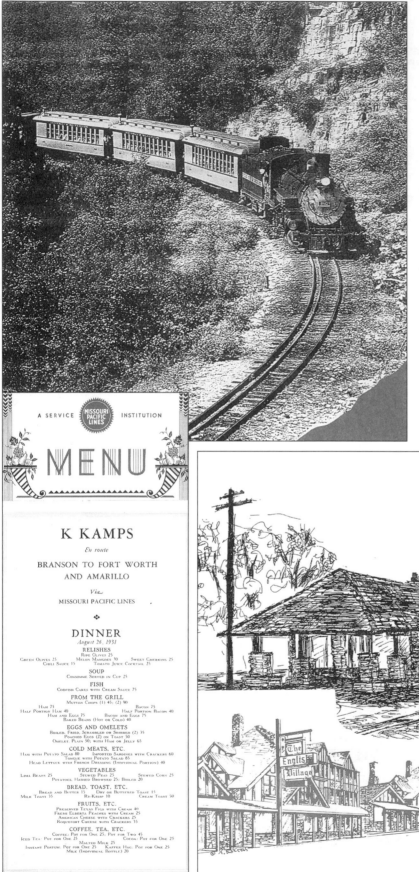

The Missouri-Pacific Train from Colorado, with stops at Amarillo, Dallas, and with its destination being Hollister, Missouri, was the transportation preferably chosen by parents for their sons to travel to Kanakuk Kamp. Roads were not in very good condition, certainly not like today's, and the train served as a convenient and safe journey for the Kampers.

Their return tickets were given to the Station Master who locked them in the depot

Kampers arrived by train, then boarded one of the steamboats for the remainder of their trip to Kamp.

safe until the end of Kamp. The Kampers were met at the Station and escorted to one of the two transportation Steamboats: "The Sadie H." or "The Virginia Mae" which were waiting at the Hollister Dock on the White River (now Lake Taneycomo). The Kampers were deboarded on the beach of Kanakuk Kamp.

The Missouri-Pacific Menu shown in the

A SERVICE MISSOURI PACIFIC LINES INSTITUTION

MENU

K KAMPS

En route

BRANSON TO FORT WORTH AND AMARILLO

Via

MISSOURI PACIFIC LINES

DINNER

August 26, 1931

RELISHES

Ripe Olives 25
Green Olives 25 Melon Mangoes 30 Sweet Gherkins 25
Chili Sauce 15 Tomato Juice Cocktail 25

SOUP

Consomme Served in Cup 25

FISH

Codfish Cakes with Cream Sauce 75

FROM THE GRILL

Mutton Chops (1) 45; (2) 90
Ham 75 Bacon 75
Half Portion Ham 40 Half Portion Bacon 40
Ham and Eggs 75 Bacon and Eggs 75
Baked Beans (Hot or Cold) 40

EGGS AND OMELETS

Boiled, Fried, Scrambled or Shirred (2) 35
Poached Eggs (2) on Toast 50
Omelet, Plain 50; with Ham or Jelly 65

COLD MEATS, ETC.

Ham with Potato Salad 80 Imported Sardines with Crackers 60
Tongue with Potato Salad 85
Head Lettuce with French Dressing (Individual Portion) 40

VEGETABLES

Lima Beans 25 Stewed Peas 25 Stewed Corn 25
Potatoes, Hashed Browned 25; Boiled 20

BREAD, TOAST, ETC.

Bread and Butter 15 Dry or Buttered Toast 15
Milk Toast 35 Ry-Krisp 10 Cream Toast 50

FRUITS, ETC.

Preserved Texas Figs with Cream 40
Fresh Elberta Peaches with Cream 25
American Cheese with Crackers 25
Roquefort Cheese with Crackers 35

COFFEE, TEA, ETC.

Coffee: Pot for One 25; Pot for Two 45
Iced Tea: Pot for One 25 Cocoa: Pot for One 25
Malted Milk 25
Instant Postum: Pot for One 25 Kaffee Hag: Pot for One 25
Milk (Individual Bottle) 20

Choo-Choo?"

pictures was used in the Dining Car in the summer. (Quite a contrast to the "McDonald's Menu" that Kampers choose from each summer when traveling in the Twenty-first century to the Kanakuk Kamps by bus or car.)

One summer when Spike was a counselor, there was a robbery at the Depot. The robbers broke into the safe and removed the contents: railroad tickets. When the Kampers heard about this, they were worried about how they would get back home without their tickets. Luckily the Station Master had combined all the Kampers' return tickets on one form, in order to conserve space in the small safe. It seemed that form was not worthy to the robbers and not stolen. Kampers were much relieved when this news was passed on to Kanakuk Kamp.

Bank Robbers Take Railroad Tickets Of 72 Texas People

The theft of seventy-two return trip railroad tickets for as many Dallas and Texas boys and girls in summer camp near Branson, Mo., failed to delay the homeward bound trip of the enthusiastic youngsters, who arrived by special Pullmans over the Texas & Pacific and Missouri Pacific Railways on Thursday morning.

Stubs for the return trip were placed in a Hollister (Mo.) bank during the camp, and a bank robbery resulted in the loss of the tickets. Railroad officials immediately issued new blanket tickets covering the safe return of all the youngsters. Three tickets in all were issued, one good for fifty children to DAllas, one for nine to Bonham and one for thirteen to Amarillo. Clarence W. Olive, assistant general agent for the Missouri Pacific, and R.P. Sellers, strict passenger agent for the Texas & Pacific, arranged the homeward trip after the loss of the original tickets.

KAMP KEMO FOR GIRLS IN 1938

Rockaway Beach

Spike and I married in Dallas, Texas. He had graduated from A&M with a BS degree in Electrical Engineering, worked at Dallas Power & Light Co. for sixteen months, and was then hired by an engineering company in Houston, Texas. He wasn't excited about working in the engineering field the rest of his life. I urged him to go back to A&M, receive a BA in Education in order to follow his dream: working with youth (which he achieved.) Then we both attended USC where he received a Masters Degree in Physical Education and Health. (Spike was prepared and on the way for a better life!)

In May 1938, we packed our meager domestic possessions, drove to College Station, stored our "loot" in the top floor of an abandoned "Ghost House" (so it was rumored) and headed for Kanakuk Kamp to spend the summer!

Uncle Bill was elated Spike would be back at Kanakuk. He had contacted his friend who had worked at Kanakuk and later started Kamp Kemo for Girls and gave me a counselor job. Kemo was located on Bull Creek, outside of Rockaway Beach.

Kamp Kemo staff and Kampers; Darnell White top row right.

1938

Second Season

June 25th to August 19th

$225.00

KE-MO KAMP

FOR GIRLS

ON

Lake Taneycomo

"In the Heart of the Ozarks"

Sister Camp

To

Kanakuk Kamp

The "K" Kamps for Boys and Girls

Dedicated

To

Character—Health—Happiness

OWNERS

MR. AND MRS. GRADY SKILLERN

Central High School

Tulsa, Okla.

1343 East 21st

Phone 4-1670

I was a Counselor there 1938 Taught Horseback Riding also in charge of Kamp Fires Thurs. Nights Spike came over in Kanakuk's boat would Dance The Indian Dances w/ me —

I stayed at Kanakuk until it was time to leave for Kamp Kemo. While we were at Kanakuk, Spike spent evenings teaching me the Indian dances and how to conduct Indian Ceremonies. Uncle Bill had an old Boat with a 25 hp motor. Spike motored down Lake Taneycomo to Bull Creek on Thursday Nights to assist me in the Indian Ceremonies. A few times, however, the old motor would break down, and Spike wouldn't make it! Our nights off coincided, and we slept in the deserted field in our sleeping bag under the romantic moon shining down. We had only been married seven months when we "went to Kamp!"

I also was hired to teach horseback riding. I could ride well, but I had never been an instructor. Spike was an optimist – "Go, girl, Go!" He convinced me that I could handle it. Spike had been in the Field Artillery in the Cadet Corps at A&M and still had his Manual which he gave me to study. At least, I learned the "talk." (When you are young and married to Spike, he could charm you into anything!) . My cabin had ten young teenage girls for the 7 week Term..Some of the girls were homesick and cried at night; I managed to lull them to sleep, then scramble up into my upper bunk and softly cried, too. I missed Spike!

Little did either of us know that our lives (and the lives of Bob, Bill, and Joe) would be in Exciting Adventures in Christian Athletics for Youth at Kanakuk Kamps.

KAMP KANAKUK

In the hills of old Missouri
On Taneycomo's shore—
Lies a spot that is beloved
In our hearts forever more.

Nestled down among blue mountains,
By a lake of Deeper hue,
Is this place that tugs the heart strings
Of both me and you and you.

There's nothing superficial
Or elegant or grand
To make one gasp with wonder
At the sights on either hand.

True—the landscape there is lovely,
In a lazy Ozark way—
And the sunsets there will thrill you
At the close of every day.

The blue hills there are restful
And the atmosphere not bad—
And as for fun and pleasure
Well, no better can be had.

But its not in seein' scenery
That our heart beats quicken up—
Its from drinkin' deep of friendship
That we love Kamp Kanakuk.

—Ed Albin.

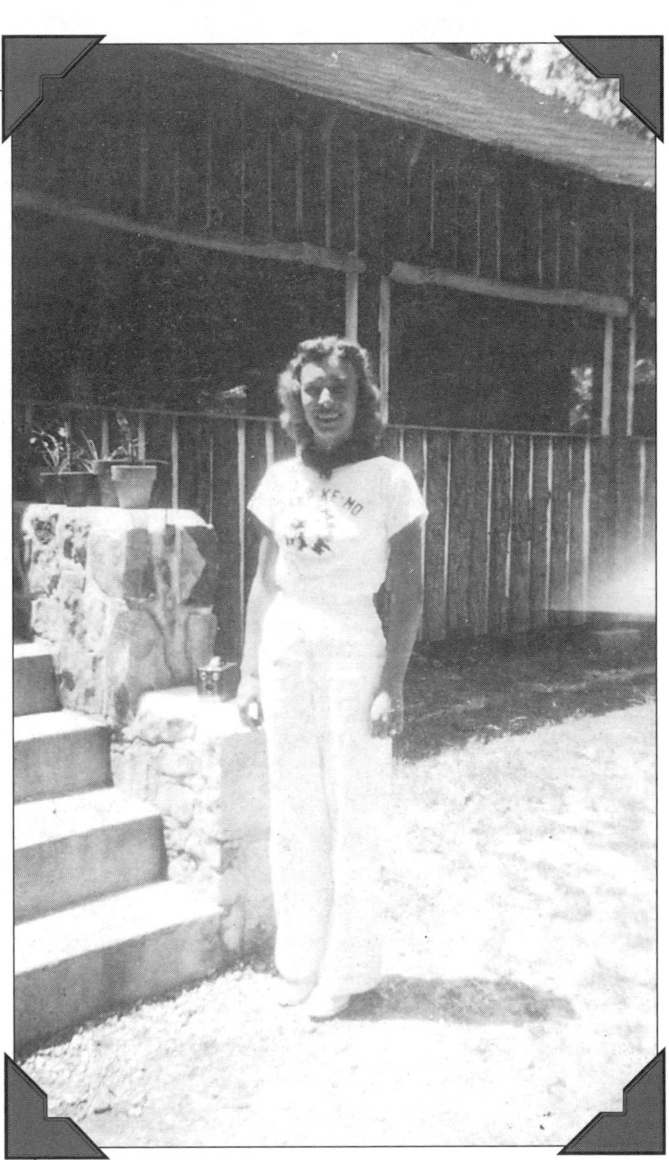

Darnell White taught horseback riding and was in charge of Kamp Kemo's ceremonies.

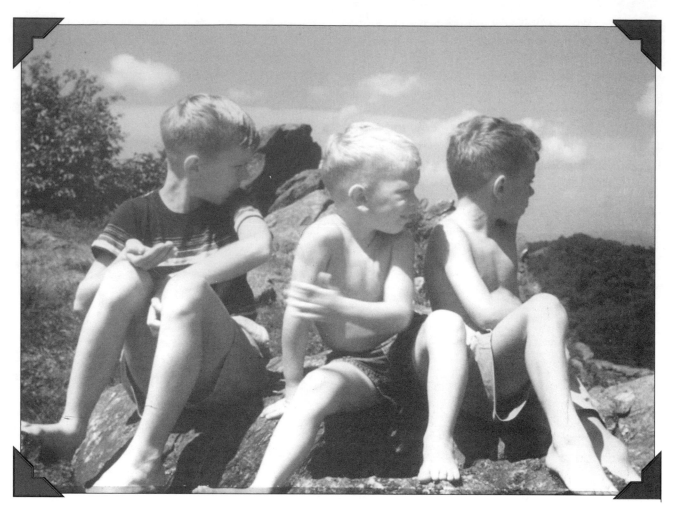

Bob, Joe and Bill White

In The Good Ole' Summertime

Spike wanted his sons to see every state in the United States, and each summer when they were a good age to travel and "see the world," our family brought Spike's dream to fruition. Seat belts were not heard of at that time. Spike converted the back end of our vehicle into a wrestling area where the boys could play games, get rid of a little energy "messing around" and each of us could have a chance to take naps. (Not unusual at all for the car to stop on the side of the road and have a round of spankings when driving long periods.) American History Books for Youth were read as we traveled. In the summers and during other holiday periods, Bob, Bill, Joe, along with Spike and me drove to and through all 48 States. (Later, Hawaii and Alaska were visited, also.)

In the summer of 1953, we traveled to Washington, DC to visit Spike's brother JoJo and his family. With their three children, the "cousins" had a big reunion together, and we visited the Capitol in all its wonder and history. On the return trip to Texas, we spent three days at Kanakuk Kamp. On our second morning, Coach Lantz and a counselor drove our family to a "put in" on the White River to float. We paddled and stopped overnight at a Long Creek gravel bar. The next day we paddled into

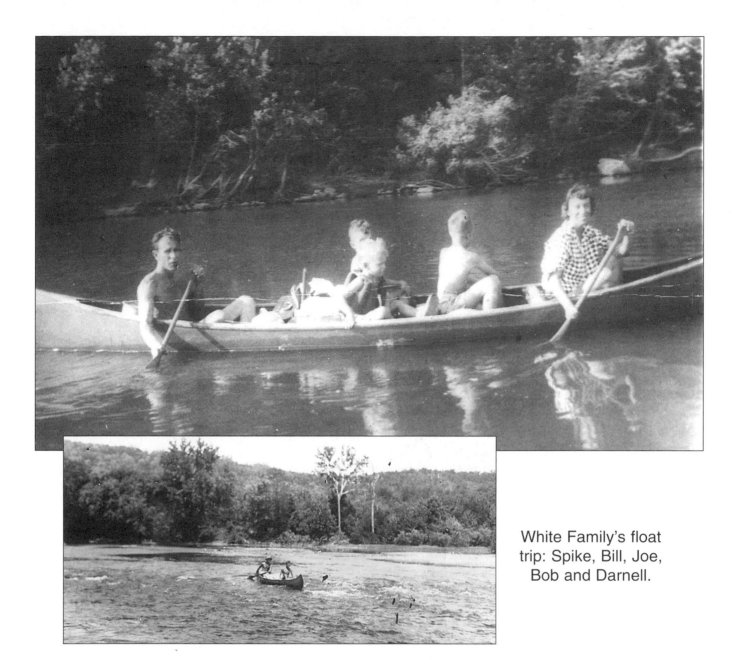

White Family's float trip: Spike, Bill, Joe, Bob and Darnell.

Kamp Kanakuk: the first float trip for our family. It was a wonderful and impressive trip for each of us. As we drove out the gate very early the next morning, "Uncle Bill" was at the gate to tell us "Goodbye." It was then that he told Spike and me that he felt compelled to sell Kamp, and that he wanted Spike to buy the Kamp. This was a surprise to us and afterward he and Spike kept in touch. I learned well then that when "Uncle Bill" prayed about anything, it would happen! Often in the years we were married, "Uncle Bill" would write us that when the time came, he wanted Spike to be the person to buy and run Kanakuk Kamp. Sometime in early fall, Spike and I decided that this was a fine opportunity and experience for our family. The only way we could afford to enroll our boys in Kanakuk Kamp was to do it: "Buy it!"

We talked with "Uncle Bill" and he suggested that we come the following summer, and get involved with Spike on staff and me in the office observing and learning the "ropes." At the end of that summer, we would purchase Kanakuk Kamp.

There were a few "old hands" who had been on Staff for years who were disappointed that Coach Lantz sold the Kamp to someone who had not been there in years; however, they had heard "Uncle Bill" at the campfires often tell "The Spike White Story" and this probably was an asset. Coach Lantz's knees were in bad shape since an automobile accident, and the walking and keeping up physically on these rugged hills were not friendly to his condition. He was much relieved, genuinely ready, and anticipated the growth and development that Kanakuk Kamp would experience with new energy and dreams that were his dreams, also.

Attending the American Camp Association Conference, I learned how to hire Office Girls, how to remember names of Staff members, parents and their progeny, how to order camp clothing in the right amounts and sizes, how to award Ribbons and Medals, and how to order groceries, take bids and work with the cooks and dining hall staff. Walsie Ray was a good-natured and fantastic cook although she often ran out of staples before telling me until it was time to prepare a meal. I urged her to let me know before the last amount was being used. Each time I asked (trying to encourage her to be responsible and independent), "How much shall I order?" With a happy and secure smile, Walsie always answered, "It takes a lot!" I gave up and counted my blessings for her cooking talents and sweet spirit.

Selecting Office Girls was a natural! In our home I conducted a class in Modeling and Manners to high school girls. My very best friend from my own teenage years in Dallas also lived in College Station. Phil and Sara June Goode's four girls and our three boys were about the same ages. Three of the Goode girls (the youngest was a Kamper at KOMO) worked in the Kamp Office.

In the month of May, Spike drove to Kamp long before school was out for the summer. My office gals and three sons drove with me to Kamp in the Kamp Station Wagon. The long 11-hour drive to these Ozarks Hills was a long, laughing, lively drive with many "pit stops" for snacks, sodas, and stretching.

Office Girls were a mainstay in the operation of Kamp. Their fresh enthusiasm made many chores light labor. They covered the gamut of out-of-the-ordinary jobs to preparing for the Opening of Kamp. Everything was a "big deal." Charts for Chiefs, Charts for Cabin Clean-up, Charts for Competition, Charts for Knot-tying, Charts for Passing Trees, Charts for Toothbrush Check-ups mostly all were done outside the Office where the Girls acquired a good start on suntans.

During Work Week, Spike gave driving lessons to the Office Girls. He taught them how to drive pick ups while using the gear-shift (no automatic cars) in these Ozark Hills, as well as the importance of staying within range behind Spike when transporting Float Trippers in the back of "Old Blue." An office girl would drive a pick-up truck loaded with camping gear and food and often pull a trailer of canoes. The Office Girls were eager, enthusiastic, excited, and ready for any errand or special trip.

Driving to the "put in" places wasn't on four-lane highways. The "shun-pike" and the narrow, hilly, rocky roads demanded a driver's concentration, and, as if that weren't enough, "keeping up with Spike was an all-time challenge." Kanakuk Kamps, in later years, owned buses for these excursions. (Erstwhile Kampers to this day brag about their adventures riding in the back of "Old Blue.")

Every summer when the Kamp photographer took pictures, the Office Gals, Jane Welch, my years-long friend and wife of Barney, and I found unique places and props ready for our picture, hoping to be selected for the Kanakuk catalog. Once Cheri Bonsteel climbed a tree to sit on the tree limb that hung over the battered old flat boat we found down in the slough. Jane, the other girls, and I were in the boat below Cherie "out on a limb." At the precise moment the picture was snapped, the limb broke and down fell Cheri in the boat, and we all swamped! We have pictures of her caught in the act!

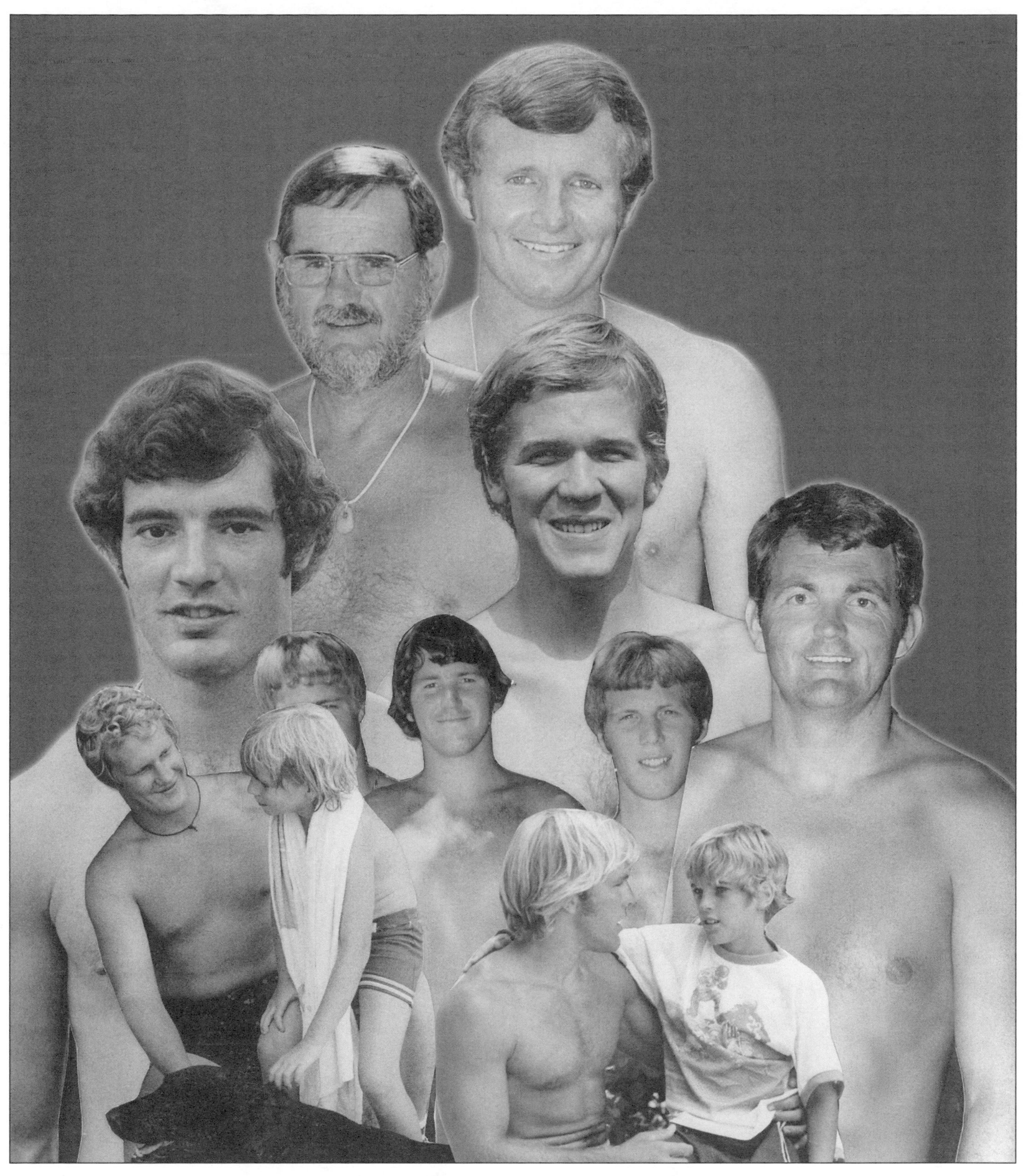

Ozzie Burk, Rocky Rockhold, Hank Harmon, David High,
Johnny Kochs, Bill Bumpas, Dick Bowles, and Jim Cunningham

THE KANAKUK HALL OF FAME
...Eternally in our Memories...

UNCLE BILL LANTZ
"FATHER OF KANAKUK"
1981

Kanakuk is following you, Uncle Bill! You said, "Live I'm Third" by putting God first, others second and yourself third. You ALWAYS did that!

You told us to live the four square life by increasing in wisdom, in stature, in favor with God, and in favor with man like Jesus did. With your living example it was easy to see how!

You always treated your body as a temple of the Holy Spirit and you loved your fellow man!

The population of Heaven has increased by tens of thousands because of Christ in you. We're forever grateful!

"I have fought a good fight, I have finished the race, I have kept the faith." II Timothy 4:7

Coach Bill Lantz's
Stop Watch
(He was never without it, most often in the palm of his hand.)

BORN IN KEARNEY, NEBRASKA, ON OCTOBER 21ST 1898. BILL WAS A THREE YEAR ALL-STATER IN BASKETBALL AND FOOTBALL AT RAVENNA, NEBRASKA. HE WAS ONE OF THE GREATEST TRACK COACHES IN OKLAHOMA HISTORY. AT TULSA CENTRAL HIGH SCHOOL, IN A 25 YEAR PERIOD, HIS TRACK TEAMS WON 15 STATE CHAMPIONSHIPS AND NEVER PLACED LOWER THAN THIRD. HIS CROSS-COUNTRY TEAMS WON 19 STATE CHAMPIONSHIPS AND HE WAS THE FOUNDER OF THE FAMED KANAKUK KAMP.

OKLAHOMA ATHLETIC HALL OF FAME

"Coach Lantz" or "Uncle Bill"

Coach Lantz is a legend in his own right to both counselors and Kampers.

Spike loved to tell the Kampers about this wonderful man: sturdy and staunch with a sterling character - a man of his word. Every morning before Kanakuk Kamp Reveille was blown for starting the day, Coach could be found at his roll-top desk in Headquarters, reading his Bible. Oh, how he loved Jesus and Paul's letters! His favorite song for Sunday church was "I Love To Tell The Story" – which he did!

After we purchased Kanakuk, Uncle Bill came back yearly to hang around a few days during Kamp, then returned to Tulsa. Because his knees were in bad shape because of a car accident, walking around these hills and up and down the switch-back trail was painful and difficult. (He used to walk down the trail on his hands!)

I still cherish every special "one-on-one" visit we had

(Con't. on Page 18)

Uncle Bill said, quietly and nostalgically, "That's just the way I always dreamed it would be."

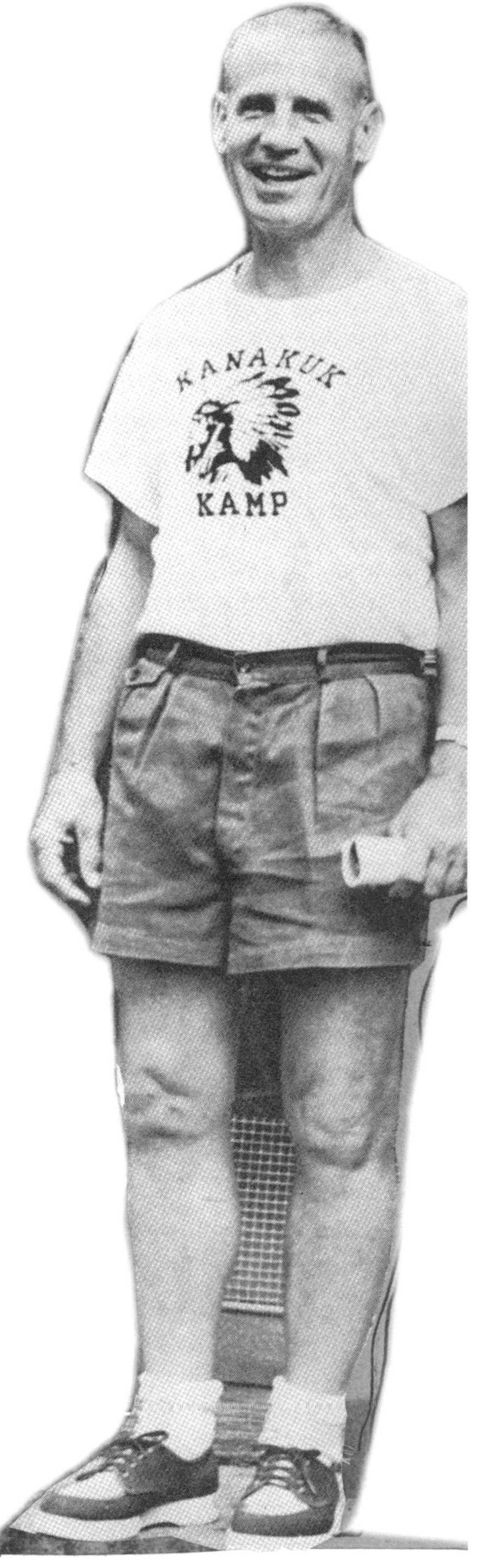

"Coach Lantz" or "Uncle Bill"

(Continued from Page 17)

together. One visit in particular comes to mind. Just the two of us were standing in back of Taneycomo Court, leaning on the rail fence, and taking a panoramic view of the lake front and the newly constructed and finished Football Field with a fine Track around it. (There had been a big mound about 150 yards in the middle of the grounds and too rolling for Sports activities.) Uncle Bill said, quietly and nostalgically, "That's just the way I always dreamed it would be." For me to have witnessed that special accolade and approval was very touching. One of the many strong traits of his mettle was encouraging others. He was a great lion of God.

Spike had many great qualities that he formed because of his association with and working under Coach Lantz at Kuggaho Camp, then later, Kanakuk Kamp. After Spike was out in the world working, Uncle Bill never forgot Spike. We learned that at Kanakuk Indian Ceremonies each summer, Uncle Bill told the "Spike White Story" and the "Davy O'Brien Story." Wish I could have heard him as he talked about Spike in that setting: all those Kampers sitting in a circle on benches watching the flaming fire scattering sparks in the air, nothing else stirring except perhaps lightening bugs and cicadas, and listening to Uncle Bill standing outside the teepee. It didn't get any better than that for kids; big kids and little kids alike!

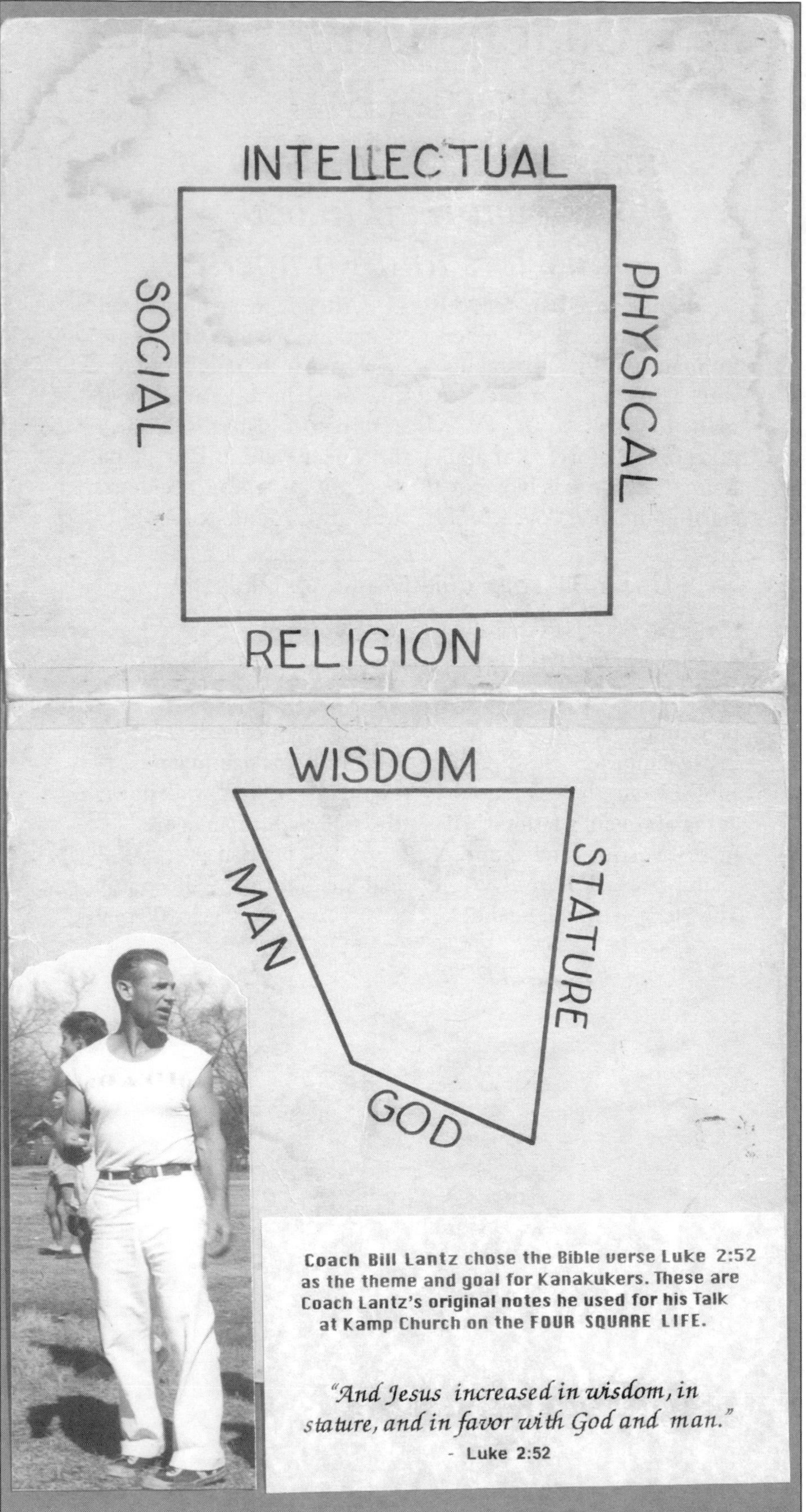

Coach Bill Lantz chose the Bible verse Luke 2:52 as the theme and goal for Kanakukers. These are Coach Lantz's original notes he used for his Talk at Kamp Church on the FOUR SQUARE LIFE.

"And Jesus increased in wisdom, in stature, and in favor with God and man."
- Luke 2:52

Council Ring
(Indian Campfire Ceremonies)

Every Saturday night, Camp Kuggaho had "Cowboy Campfires" – counselors and campers sitting around a campfire singing and story-telling. (Oddly enough, that same location is where K-Kountry started their first church service when it opened years later.) Back in the year 1926, the narrow old dirt narrow road from Branson ran right across the Cowboy Campfire. Only a few cars, trucks, and horses passed by on the road that dead-ended into the White River.

When Coach Lantz took over the Camp Kuggaho, he asked Spike to find a new location to set up an Indian (in lieu of "Cowboy") Camp across the road from the KUK entrance. Spike discovered a dense wooded area: an ideal size and shape for the Council Ring. Spike and his good friend Loris Moody chopped, cut, and cleared all trees except the natural circle of Cedar trees on the outward ring. Since 1933, this Council Ring which hosts Indian Talks, with the beating of tom-toms while Chiefs and tribesmen dancing genuine Indian Dances have been a special and meaningful experience.

The same tradition is perpetuated today. After sunset, in darkness and silence, Counselors lead the Kampers by cabins (only counselors carry flash-lights) as they walk single file across the road, up the hill, and across to the dark bare circle. In all solemnity, the Kampers sit on the elevated benches with their cabins and counselors at designated places. After everyone is settled (still in silence), an awesome, almost magical flaming fire flashes upward from the center rock-mound, lighting up the Ring (no human is seen to have set the fire!). The Indian Ceremony begins with apt attention from the mesmerized Kampers.

Kanakomo Kamp for Girls, beginning in 1958, for several years had their own Council Ring just across the road East of the

(Continued on page 20)

(Continued from page 19)
Girls' Tennis Courts, in the woods; however, they now use the Original Council Ring at Kanakuk, only on another night.

Two of my fondest memories are the first time watching Spike and Joe do the Hoop Dance together, and then later, to see Debbie Jo join Spike performing the Hoop Dance at the Girls' Campfire.

The Hoop Dance is competitive, and starts out slowly. One Indian challenges another to dance through his (or her) own hoop to the beat of the tom-tom, getting faster and faster until one of the dancers is exhausted. Each hoop is not much bigger around than the dancer's body. Dancing to the beating tom-tom, not tripping on the hoop as it is danced through and over the head, down the body, and out again, over and over, and faster and faster, requires much practice and perseverance.

Spike White standing
teepee painted by Ed Alirn.

Work Week At Camp

Spike carried 3"x5" cards with job instructions to be handed out when the Staff met at Taneycomo Court after breakfast to go over the schedule of the day. Groups were organized with instructions given on the cards that Spike made. In the old building across from "old Mess," tools and work gloves and other necessities were laid out, ready for the groups to select.

I was told of this particular happening: Spike cruised around in his truck in order to observe the work being performed. He came upon a few counselors leaning on their hoe-handles as they talked and laughed. They were completely oblivious to Spike's truck parking nearby. There hadn't been any change in the area, it was still in dire need of being cleared of fallen limbs and debris. Spike got out of the truck, reached into his tool chest removed a saw, and walked to the cozy huddle of counselors. He took a hoe from each counselor, sawed a foot off each of the hoe handles, handed them back and said, "You can't separate from your work on a long handle until your handle is short enough to bend your back close to your work"... and walked off, got in his truck and drove away.

"Honest suntan is on your back; laziness in on your stomach."

On another occasion, Spike discovered a few counselors sunbathing instead of working. Spike's short comment to the loafers was, "Honest suntan is on your back; laziness is on your stomach." With that bit of wisdom, he drove away. I am sure the counselors were up working muy pronto, and probably remembered Spike's few words a long time.

Work Week At Camp

(Continued from Page 21)

Traditions are many splendid things in each of our lives. They bind and they remind. At Kanakuk there are many traditions, and not one of us – not the Kampers who came back summer after summer, nor the Staff, would have been disappointed if the familiar and faithful "we always... traditions" were not done the same way each summer.

At 10:30 a.m. and 3:00 p.m., during Work Week, each Staff-work crew assembled at the Dining Hall for tall glasses of iced tea, no matter the job assignments nor the locations on the Kamp grounds. The camaraderie and laughter, along with the exaggerated stories of the work assignments, the blisters, backaches, scrapes and pain were expanded and shared. The counselors' vigor and vitality returned as if a magic wand waved over their tired and tested stamina. The "Old Hands" loved to "egg" and tease the Rookie Staff relentlessly.

"Iced Tea-Times" helped to make men out of boys!

"Dusties"

If you remember "dusties," then you go back "a fer piece." During Work Week, after the raking, scrapping, painting, mowing, hauling, washing down and scouring the bunks and cabins, "Old Mess" spiffed up and shining, awnings installed, "St. Louis" sanitized, Tribal charts made for the Summer, and the "Bag Swing" stuffed with sawdust and hung on the venerable Elm Tree in back of "Old Mess," then it was time for "Old Blue" to be driven down 65-S. on the way to Harrison, Arkansas, around Omaha. There would be an obnoxious and merry group of counselors gathered to send off the "first crew" and to yell out challenges and bad luck and "voodoos" on the first shovelers.

"Some of the crew were Rookies and overwhelmed at the fanfare as they didn't have a clue what all the hoop-la was about. The "Oldies" were fired up and eager to prepare them for this maiden voyage."

The "Timer" was at the Gate to record the time of departure to give the "Set, Go!" to the driver of "Old Blue" and Crew. The back of the truck would be covered with tarps and canvases, and each counselor and his heavy wide shovel. Some of the crew were Rookies and were overwhelmed at the fanfare as they didn't have a clue what all the hoop-la was about. The "Oldies" were fired up and eager to prepare them for this maiden voyage.

The destiny of the trip would take them to a sawmill where huge mounds of "dusties" (wood shavings/sawdust) would be ready for removal. "Dusties" were important to Kamp. Rocky paths and grounds on Kanakuk where Kampers ran, walked, fell, and played would be padded all summer by the sheer magic of those "dusties." It made a definite difference and protected Kampers from skinned elbows, knees and shins that would possibly prevent a Kamper from having a good summer or being able to contribute to the sports activities and help his Tribe.

The Crew gave their muscles, heart, and ernest endeavors as fast as they could shovel with the long handled shovel, filling the truck, jumping in back atop the treasure, and returning to Kanakuk where the "Timer" waited at the Gate to announce the length of time of trip, start to finish.

Each "haul of dusties" would be dumped out in piles at designated areas. There was much drama watching the routine: apple peck-baskets were used to scoop up the "dusties" to spread and cushion the rough grounds - under the chinning bar, the ropes, the bag-swing, the paths from the road, and down paths to each cabin.

In the meantime, the second Crew with canvases, tarps, and shovels were loaded in the back of the truck and waved off by the "Timer" at the Gate. The driver (usually Spike) always drove at the same speed. Sounds silly, but you had to experience it to appreciate the camaraderie and seriousness of the competition of the "dusties" for Kanakuk Kamp.

"Everything's a 'Big Deal'" was Kanakuk's logo!

In Back of "Old Mess"

There was something unique and gripping about the back of "Old Mess" to the Kamp and counselors in those long-ago days at Kanakuk. There was a "bag swing" that hung from the long, sturdy, staunch trunk of a very old American Elm tree, close to the back side of Old Mess. Kampers could straddle the top of the sawdust-loaded gunny sack tied-at-the-top securely, wrap his legs and feet around the seat, and swing way out and beyond, hit the building with an extended foot again, and soar with eyes closed. The inevitable that some Kamper would not pass by a quick jump on the bag swing when he was on the way to meet at Taneycomo Court or to a meal. The "Bag-Swing" probably was cherished and recalled as much as any of the popular and beloved places at Kamp. "Oh, to go back and be a boy at Kamp again!"

> "It's better than new; it's been used."
>
> *Ora Dickey*

The Bag-Swing had two personalities with two different Kanakuk groups. After Taps and after Kampers had dropped off to sleep, several pinpoint lights could be seen coming from different directions down through the Cabin area. The cool night air and the silent darkness were interrupted by the crunching of feet on gravel and soon the air was quiet as a mouse again, except for whisperings around the bag-swing. Then, there was only one little light of a flash-light shining on an opened Bible, and ever-so-dimly, reflections of faces in a circle. Jim Welch's voice softly reading "LETTERS OF PAUL." Joe White was a Junior Counselor and became a "born-again Christian" at the beloved Bag-Swing. I often wondered how many others were saved around that dear tattered and dirty bag-swing behind "Old Mess." As Ora Dickey, a humorous and authentic "hill-billy" maintenance man would say, "It's better than new; it's been used."

LOWERING THE FLAG AT SUNSET

SUNSHINE CABIN
KUGGAHO KAMP
BRANSON, MO
1949
THE BUGLERS
KUGGAHO KAMP
1931

The Ropes and the Chinning Bar
At The Side Of "Old Mess"

The small area between the side and back of "Old Mess" was an active and lively place, especially before and after breakfast. Tooth-brushing was three times a day for everyone after each meal. The Chiefs were there with their Tribal Charts to check off each Kamper when he brushed his teeth. Outside "St. Louis" (and I don't know how the bath house was given that handle!) were individual boxes, one for each Kamper with his name, and one for each counselor. Before breakfast, after Reveillee was sounded by the Bugler, every Cabin lined up to climb the huge 1" by 25ft. ropes, eight-in-a-row in the early '60's, whereas there had been four, hanging from a bar. Skinny and not-so-skinny bodies lined up to climb as high as their imagination and determination would take them.

The Chinning Bar was built at Kamp by Spike in the '50's. It became a popular apparatus and was also part of the Morning Wake-up Action before breakfast. (I can picture Spike teaching the kips and feats of the chinning bar to one and all. In our home in College Station, our sons suite of three beds, three desks, three individual closets, and an open space for ping pong and weights, Spike hung a chinning bar the width of a closet door and height high enough for chinning without feet dragging.)

Bob White recently told me a story about Spike and the Chinning Bar at Kamp. He and Spike were walking together to check on repairs. Without breaking a stride, Spike jumped up, grabbed the bar and did a couple of giant swings and a gainer, dismounted, fell in step with Bob, and went on down the switchback trail to the lake front.

Another story that Jim Cunningham shared with me happened around 1972 when Jim was first hired. Spike was giving Jim a tour of the Kamp, walking and talking as they were passing the Weight Lifting room where Joe was instructing at the Chinning Bars. As Jim and Spike stopped to observe, Joe called to Spike, "Do something on the bar, Dad." Spike didn't say a word. He approached the bar, wiped chalk dust on palms of his hands, and without a break, skipped up to the bar, did a giant swing, went into a dismount with a neat fly-away, then quietly aside said to Joe, "Don't ever ask me to do that again." Spike had not used the bar in several years.

Spike was a disciplined and fun-loving fellow. He loved to install FUN places for "kids." The Ropes Courses, Zip Lines and Slides have Spike written all over them. Spike attended Outward Bound, Young Life Camp in North Carolina, Kayaked at Nantahala, the ten best White Waters in the USA, and the Grand Canyon. He passed his fun and exciting knowledge to Kamp's Programs.

Walking to Marvel Cave - Silver Dollar City

One of the trips started by Coach Lantz was the all-day, all-Kamp, all-walk to Silver Dollar City and Marvel Cave (decades ago). Walking to Silver Dollar City was a highlight and a memorable experience for Kanakuk Kampers and Staff.

However, when the city of Branson grew larger, and the narrow roads improved and widened for the growing traffic because of theaters built by famous celebrities, restaurants, and stores on 76 Hwy, the "Walks" were history!

After breakfast, the senior Kampers and counselors were first to walk out the Gate: destination SDC. "No stopping for water or loitering, and stay on the side of the road." (Actually, it was rare to see many cars on the 14-mile trek)." Some senior-division Kampers were track-runners and in shape; they were allowed to proceed at their own pace to arrive at the picnic area at SDC, just across the road from the entrance. As each individual arrived, a designated counselor announced his "time" to the final destination. Water, of course, was a welcome item. The communication all the rest of the day was, "How far did you go?" and "What was your 'time'?"

In the meantime, the junior division followed out the Kamp Gate, and the Midget Division always stayed just behind with Head Counselor Barney Welch along side the last Kamper. (I can still "see" Barney bringing up the rear, carrying his cane whittled from a cedar tree on a Mystery Truck Trip.) Kids, big and small, adored Barney: great athlete in college, fun to be around, loved kids, encouraged them, a true leader! Counselors were always challenging Barney and desired most to beat him in all sports to no avail! Great Kamp Guy!

Finally, forty-five minutes from the time the Midget Division departed, "Big Blue" (the trusty Kanakuk truck with cattle-guard rails) with Spike at the helm, drove out the Gate. Along the road, Spike made many stops, picking up groups or single Kampers, first calling out how many miles each one had walked! The women-folks of Kamp joined Barney and his group (no contenders for a record) walking. I chose to walk with "Little Joe" and made it to the Municiple Air Field, 6 miles. The next and last summer with Joe, the mileage was 10 miles. "Heart-break Hill" around Dewey Bald had "done me in."

Letter from Jack Herschend

Dear Darnell,

May 25, 2007

Jamie Jo has given me a wonderful opportunity to think back, with head and heart, about Spike.

First memories are of a young Spike who loved exploring Marvel Cave. We became friends in 1950. Spike brought hundreds of Kampers to the cave and it was my privilege to be their guide. Spike accompanied me on almost every trip.

A few years later Spike started the "tradition" of boys running from K-1 to Marvel Cave. (The traffic on Hwy. 76 was much lighter in those days.) Spike would pick up those who could not complete the run in the original "Old Blue." Boys would stand up in the back of the truck and as far as I know no one was ever hurt.

My last memory was hearing my best friend, now old and bent, describing his love for you. There was a glow and a beautiful smile on his face as he described your "love affair."

In the over 50 years I knew Spike and the many rivers and caves we enjoyed together, never did I ever hear a word about his bride that wasn't honoring. What a great lesson he taught me, a younger husband.

And in between the earliest and the last memory were hundreds of awesome memories. I learned soooo much and laughed so much. I remember his warm humor, i.e. he asked me on one occasion "Jack, tell me something, when did I go from good looking to looking good?" He went on to say how folks look into the casket at a funeral and say, "He's looking good.", i.e. he walked into our newly completed home and said, "Jack, this to too good for who it's for."

Spike wasn't handsome but was beautiful; somehow he smiled with his entire face, such warmth.

It was such a privilege to call Spike "best friend." He was the best mentor a younger man could ever have.

We slept many nights in a tent along a river. Spike always kneeled beside his sleeping bag to speak to his Lord. His faith so simple; so profound. As he prayed my faith grew.

Darnell, my friend, thank you for sharing him with us.

Love, Jack

Barbers and Tutors go to Kamp

"Summertime and the living is easy" – so the song goes. And summertime when boys are away from home, in a sports Kamp for eight weeks, the need for haircuts was essential. Coach Lantz never approved the boys' hair to be longer and hanging over the top of a shirt collar, definitely no hanging down in the face over the eyes, and absolutely no long sideburns or ponytails. After Coach Lantz left, the barber from town continued to make a trip to Kanakuk every four weeks. In the MAT FLAT (Wrestling and Boxing Arena), a straight chair would be set up for the barber from town, and each boy whose name was on the list was called. Most of the boys were okay with it; however, some boys arrived at Kamp with long hair even though they knew the rules. Their parents just sent them to Kamp and let Coach or Spike deal with it. Kampers were not the only ones, however. A few Counselors tried to get by without a needed haircut, but the rules were the same for everyone. The barber earned his charge of "four-bits" a head. It was no problem in the long run: Kampers joined together and bonded in the sports activities, having made friends, sharing in the cabin, being accepted, laughing and learning to be free and uncluttered from the outside world's peer pressure.

A straight chair would be set up … and each boy whose name was on the list was called… The Barber earned his charge of "four-bits" a head.

Another out-of-the-ordinary Kanakuk adjustment was the need for a tutor at Kamp for some of the Kampers.

Because the one eight-week Term at Kanakuk each summer took up most of the time out of school, some boys and girls who regularly attended Kamp needed to go to Summer School. Due to this Spike arranged to have a tutor work with the Kampers. This served its purpose with the Bonus of Christian sports activities, adventures and experiences.

Much later, when the economy was better, there began an influx of family-traveling with more attractions. Enrollment for the next summer (often filling by late autumn) and the Waiting List too long to include. Spike made the decision that two terms would give more opportunities for more Kampers to have a Kanakuk-Kanakomo experience. Two terms, one 5-week term and one 4-week term, opened by the middle '60's.

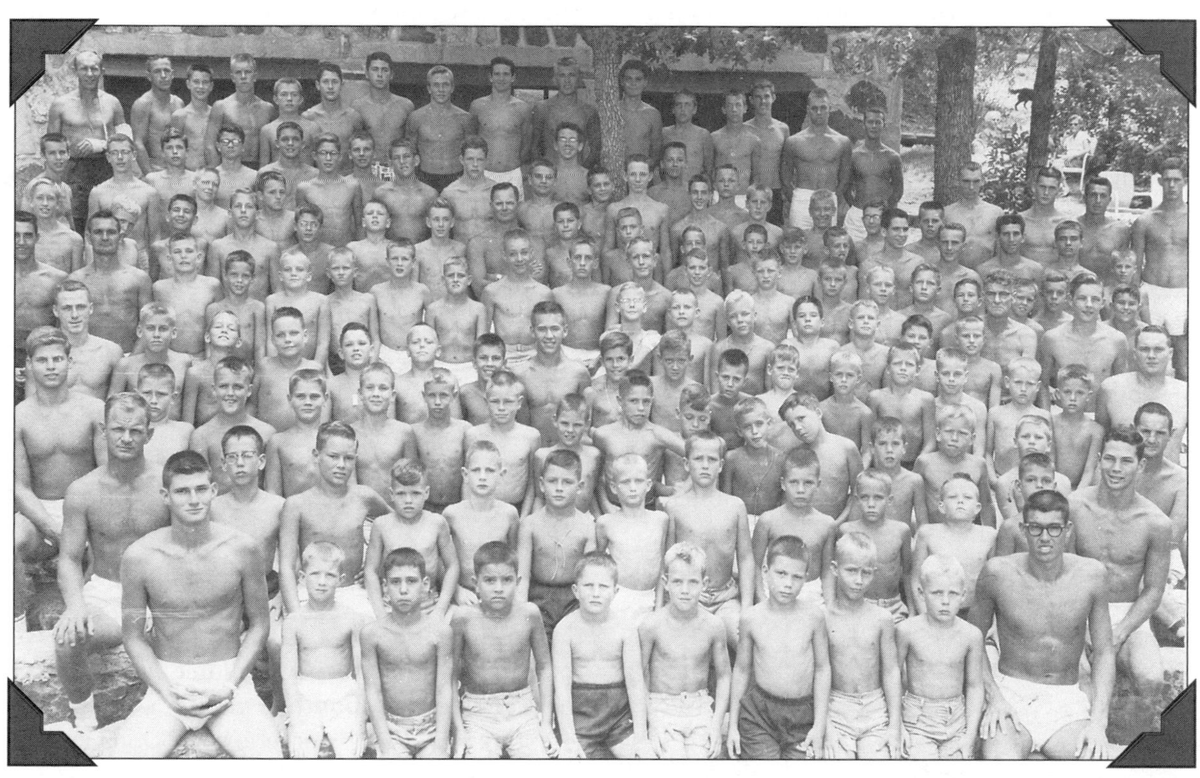

"Looking Back"

The Kanakuk Kamps of today are a stretch of the imagination from the "way we were." When Spike and I, as owners, entered the Gate of Kanakuk Kamp, we moved into the "office, bedroom, parlor, and sink" under the same roof: 24'x33'! The entrance opened to the counter, office space, and Kamp Store. Behind that wall was a fireplace (for winter or early spring), a bed (a rod dropped down from the ceiling around the bed area with curtains to be pulled for privacy (?), a small restroom with a 28" opening (sans door), commode, shower head and never-hot-water! On the roof above the 4'x5' shower stall, there was a tank. When the days were hot, perhaps the water tank would warm up for a shower; otherwise, it was cold water. There was no closet for clothes. Mold on our shoes and the like was a nuisance until I learned to put shoes in the mid-day sun weekly! "Ain't camping fun!"

In the meantime, the cabins (before Spike could repair and rebuild new cabins) had no fans, just ventilation openings on either end of each cabin. The bath house did have hot water! There were few buildings: "Old Mess" (kitchen and dining hall), wrestling- boxing "Mat Flat" and "Ping Pong Palace." When there were long rainy days, too wet to be on the sports fields, the Kampers and counselors spent time in their cabins. Card games, Tic Tac Toe, and Checkers were played to fill the time until the sun came out. Counselors and Kampers, for sure, had doses of "Cabin Fever" after the novelty and change in schedule wore off. Scuffling, "horse-play" and getting rough caused a plethora of "points off," and that meant reducing points on the Tribal Charts (which resulted in other young Braves and Chiefs being disgruntled and rightfully so)!

Darnell in the office.

Even on sunny days, many Kamper boys were given "points off" because they couldn't resist throwing small rocks and pebbles found on the paths and grounds; that's tempting stuff to an energetic boy! "Don't run!" was often heard (rocky paths played havoc on knees and arms!)

It wasn't too many summers before a gym was built at Kanakomo and a Dome was constructed over the basketball courts at Kanakuk. In addition there were improved cabins with porches and circulating fans, and a new Dining Hall, which made "Old Mess" another covered building. The Kamp facilities were finally improving and expanding.

Those days at Kamp, the "war stories' told about swamping on float trips, tents and gear soaked, rainy periods staying in the cabins extra time, the inconveniences, the lessons learned how to "make friends and influence Staff" were probably the best memories of Kanakuk Kamp, and even the "Remember-whens," points off and other goof-offs create laughter and damp eyelids!

Not a summer goes by that several Kanakukers (male and female) don't drop in to visit and talk about "those times." Their Kamp summers are cherished and re-lived through their own progeny, grand and great grandchildren. Like TAMU's philosophy, "Once an Aggie, always an Aggie," no matter the ages or number of years of yore: "Once a Kanakuker, always a Kanakuker!"

"You Don't Have To, You Get To!"
(One of many Spike-isms)

Spike taught me many things. He taught me how to make Indian Breech Cloths and Ceremonial Aprons for the Chiefs to wear at Opening and Closing Final Ceremonies, how to make moccasins for Joe and Spike for dancing, and how to design and sew the Indian Dresses for the Princesses. He also taught me how to make the Indian Beadwork on a loom for belts, bands, and other decorative accessories.

During the fall, winter, and spring, our sons helped when we used the ditto machine in the College Chapel on Campus. With the copies we would then fold the pages for the mailing of the Kanakuk Newsletters to Kampers and staff. After our first few years. when the boys were older and at the close of the summer, Spike showed the boys and me how to shingle the roof of the new addition to the Nurses' Station and Hospital. Spike said it wasn't a big roof and would be easy to shingle. (I thought it was! I resigned after that feat and performed other chores on foot!) Bob, Bill, and Joe learned a lot more about tools and how to use them than they ever wanted to know.

Every summer before the Table Rock Dam was completed, our beach would be in dire need of cleaning. The "bottom" was often flooded in the springtime and the debris piled on the bank of the lake. It was a yearly chore on Bob, Bill, and Joe's list of duties. One of Spike's oft sayings was:

"WHEN ONE WORKS, EVERYBODY WORKS"

Spike's "Ism's" were heard around Kamp often. Like "family jokes," Kanakuk Staff and Kampers picked up and quoted the Spike-isms:

"JUST A TEN MINUTE JOB"

"IT'S BETTER THAN NEW – IT'S BEEN USED"

"YOU'LL BE BETTER WIVES
AND BETTER MOTHERS"

"DARNELL, NOW LISTEN!"

"THAT'S DUMB!"

"IT'S A BEAUTIFUL DAY IN THE OZARKS"

"IT'S NOT DIFFICULT UNLESS YOU THINK IT IS"

"WHEN THINGS GET TOUGH, KNEEL"

"GOD DON'T MAKE NO JUNK"

"YOU DON'T HAVE TO, YOU GET TOO"

How Firm The Foundation

The Staff in any camp for youth is a major part of its support and success. It takes Blue-Ribbon ingredients in a Staff to make the "right stuff!" The Directors of the Kanakuk Kamps strive to hand-pick, study, and pray about applicants before hiring them. This is part of Kamp's "Seal of Approval for Good-Kamp Keeping." Caring, selfless, sensitive counselors are key ingredients,

> Chinning on the Parallel Bar behind "Old Mess" became a popular exercise for Staff and Kampers, all because of the enthusiasm Frank demonstrated.

just as the crazy, creative, controlled extroverts are who bring out the introverts with laughter and light-heartiness in everyone. Then stir in the solid, staunch, and dependable servants and mix all together to make a firm foundation.

Frank English, one of the Clown Divers, was an outstanding counselor. Like so many Kampers in the early days, Frank and his three brothers, Merrill, Pete, and Alan, "grew up" in Kamp, attending every summer's 8-week Term. Kamp was their second "Home." Their wonderful mom raised them alone. Frank and Pete were counselors later.

Frank had a ritual he honored seven days a week called "Doing My Chinnies." He was small in stature with great strength and muscles in his upper body. He installed a chinning bar between the posts of the upper and lower Bunk in Cabin Seven, where he was counselor. He chinned a wallop of a number every day without fail. When he was on the float trips, Frank would carry his chinning bar, find a couple of trees just far enough apart and install his chinning bar! Frank's routine and discipline fascinated the Kampers! Chinning on the parallel bar behind "Old Mess" became a popular exercise for staff and Kampers, all because of the enthusiasm Frank demonstrated. Spike soon took up the teaching and performing on the Bar after Frank moved on to California to teach. (Spike didn't, however, install a chinning bar at the end of our bed.)

Mike Ritchey played a lively guitar and sang "It Is No Secret" and "Just A Closer Walk With Thee" like no one else. Mike and Bill White each were dubbed "the growd" because they traveled "light." Each carried a syrup can holding his gear and wore a string with his toothbrush hanging around his neck. They were packed and ready for the River!

Mike's joie de vivre was contagious, and everyone loved him. Mike, Rocky, and Bob White made up the Team that Spike chose for the Dads and Sons' Salmon River Alaskan Float Trip after Kamp closed one year. It was a great adventure and unanimously proclaimed "Best Trip Ever."

Steve Haas was another outstanding counselor. He was there for the kids and made the summer memorable. I can see him now during Optional Period after supper, standing on the top Rocks of the Fountain, playing "Simon Says" with a plethora of Kampers. It was counselors like Steve using a free-time, a time not scheduled for him to be on duty, to perk up and give extra laughter and fun to the Kampers' Kamp experience. Blue Ribbon Counselors at Kanakuk and Kanakomo are endless. Their dedication and devotion still shines.

Frank English wrote this to me (via E-Mail):

August 16, 2006

Dear Darnell:

It's difficult to sift through all those wonderful years of Kanakuk Kamps and decide which prank was the best. However, this is about a Float Trip episode during Kamp.

During one of the 10-day float trips, word was circulated that we had not heard from the float trippers and concern was being talked about around Kamp. This was causing everyone concern and was purposely discussed at mealtimes. Frank and Spike kept the Kampers reminded by mentioning and commenting on it in the Mess Hall. Somehow we received word that Trippers would attempt to communicate with us "by carrier pigeon." We were not sure if the pigeons being sent were "homing-pigeons" or some wild variety that would not know where Kanakuk was located. That created more anxiety. Therefore, I spent dinner time on the roof of the Mess Hall with a shot gun waiting and watching for the pigeon and the message. When I would spy a suspicious bird flying overhead, I would cry out "Here comes the Messenger Bird." All the little feet within the Mess Hall would rush to the Lake Taneycomo side of the building to get a glimpse of the bird. The suspense kept building up all week. Toward the end of the week, "The Bird" did arrive! From the roof I fired the shotgun and skillfully knock the bird from the sky; I tossed the bird over the side for all to see. I quickly descended to the ground, retrieved the note and delivered it to Spike to read with gusto and much ado. The drama was talked about and written home about the rest of the summer.

Don't know if this is a memory that you would care to use, but it is one I will always remember with fondness. Spike so loved a good prank. Must be one of the reasons he was so deeply loved by us all.

Love and blessings,

Frank English

The man who matched

Captain John Ferrier's final act was a deed

Out of the sun, packed in a diamond and flying as one, the Minute Men dove at nearly the speed of sound toward a tiny emerald patch on Ohio's unwrinkled crazy quilt below.

It was a little after 9 in the morning of June 7th, 1958, and the target the Air National Guard's jet precision team was diving at was the famed Wright-Patterson Air Force Base, just outside Dayton.

On the ground, thousands of faces looked upward as Col. Walt Williams, leader of the Denver-based Sabrejet team, gauged the high-speed pullout. Guests of honor at the airshow this morning were the members of the class of '59, U.S. Military.

For the civilians who watched, the corps de ballet perfection of the red Sabre acro-team was a thing of awe and wonder. For the Minute Men pilots, Walt Williams, Capt. Bob Cherry, Lt. Bob Odle, Capt. John Ferrier, and Major Win Coomer, it was routine. They had given their show hundreds of times before several million people from Spokane, Wash., to Jacksonville, Fla., and from Burlington, Vt., to Honolulu, showing the people of the United States how proficient a reserve unit can be, telling with speed and thrills and swift smoke-strokes across the sky the Air National Guard story. For the Minute Men this was just another show, but they were glad the crowd was good, the skies were clear, and the air was morning-smooth.

Low across the fresh green grass the jet team streaked, far ahead of the planes' own noise.

????? pressed the microphone button on top his throttle: "Smoke on — now."

Then the diamond of planes was pulling straight up into the turquoise sky, a bushy tail of white smoke pluming out behind the formation.

The crowd gasped when the four shops suddenly separated, rolling to the four points of the compass and leaving a beautiful, smoky fleur de lis inscribed on the background blue of the sky.

This was the Minute Men's famed "flower burst" maneuver. For a minute the crowd relaxed, gazing at the tranquil beauty of the huge white flower that had grown from the verdant Ohio grasslands to fill the great bowl of sky.

Out on the end of his arm of the flower, Colonel Williams turned his Sabre hard, cut off the smoke trail, and dropped the rose of his F-86 to pick up speed for the low-altitude cross-over maneuver. Then, glancing back over his shoulder, he froze.

Far across the sky to the east, John Ferrier's plane was rolling. He was in trouble. And his plane was headed right for the small town of Fairborn, on the edge of Patterson field. In a moment the lovely morning turned to horror. Everyone saw. Everyone understood. One of the planes was out of control.

Racing his Sabre in the direction of the crippled plane, Colonel Williams raised his ???? There was still plenty of time, still plenty of room. Twice more Williams issued the command. Each time he was answered by a blip of smoke. He got the sense of it immediately. John Ferrier couldn't reach the mike button on the throttle because he had both hands tugging on a control stick that was locked full-throw right. But the smoke button was on the stick, and he was answering the only way he could — squeezing it to tell Walt he thought he could pull out... that he couldn't let his airplane go into the houses of Fairborn.

Capt. John T. Ferrier's Sabrejet hit the ground equidistant from four houses. There was hardly any place other than that one backyard garden where he could have hit without killing people.

There was a tremendous explosion which knocked a woman and several children to the ground. But no one was hurt — with the exception of Captain Ferrier. He was killed instantly.

Major Win Coomer, who had flown with Ferrier for years, both in the Air National Guard and on United Air Lines, and had served a combat tour with him in Korea, was the first Minute Man to land at Patterson AFB after the crash. He got a car and raced to the crash scene.

He found a neighborhood still stunned from the awful thing that had happened. There was no resentment as is ordinarily the case when a peaceful community is torn by a crash. A steady stream of people came up to tall, handsome, graying Win Coomer who stood — still in his flying suit — beside the smoking, gaping hole in the ground where his best friend had died. And, humbly, they all said the same thing: This man died for us.

our mountains

of unforgettable courage and sacrifice

"A bunch of us were standing together, watching the show," an elderly man told Coomer, "when he started to roll. He was headed straight for us. For a second I felt that we looked right at each other." There were tears in the man's eyes. "Then he pulled up right over us and put it in... there."

Ferrier's teammates figured he used the plane's rudders to steer the crippled plane away from the people and houses.

It was a bold and courageous last act. But it was not an act alien to the nature of John T. Ferrier, who had been awarded for risking his life "beyond the call of duty" in Korea to fly cover over a downed Marine pilot until helicopter rescue could come. On that sortie the pilot's own fellow flyers had been afraid to fly down into the hell of flak and ground fire to keep the Communist ground troops from the downed airman. Ferrier and a fellow Air Force flier had taken their F-51's down voluntarily and "capped" the pilot until help had come, even though Ferrier had limped home with a rocket hole "as big as Korea" in his wing.

Denverites remembered Johnny Ferrier as an outstanding Colorado University "scatback" in football, as an All-City softball player, and as an A.A.U. champion handball player — and a wonderful family man who neither smoked nor drank (his worst expletives were "dad-gum" or "dad-burn it").

The number of cars in his funeral procession was the largest in the memory of the people who attended. Traffic was halted for miles. Many people came who had never known John Ferrier, but who out of respect to the memory of a man who died a real hero.

In a letter to John Ferrier's widow, Gov. Steve McNichols of Colorado wrote: "I know that you and your children can always be proud, as we are of the fact that in his last moments he used his skill and his concern for humanity to protect others from this terrible mishap."

There were other letters of comfort for Tulie Ferrier and the three Ferrier children. Brig. Gen. Donald L. Hardy, commander of Wright-Patterson, said: "Eyewitness reports indicate that the plane was headed directly for people and houses in the area, and that a definite attempt was made by your husband to miss them. May you find comfort in the fact that his attempt was successful."

A Dayton housewife wrote: "My prayer, 'Please God, let there be a parachute,' went unanswered as I saw a burst of flame behind the trees. For this was a brave man who preferred to guide his plane into an open space away from his fellow man rather than save himself and chance the death of others."

General Thomas D. White, chief of the U.S. Air Force, wrote: "May the thought of your husband's faithfulness to his country bring increasing comfort to you as time passes."

U.S. Sen. Gordon Allott said: "His skill, both as a member of the Minute Men and as a United Airlines pilot, has been a credit to himself and his family. His shining heroism in the split second over Ohio will serve as a constant example to all of us."

It was Senator Allott who called long-distance from Washington on September 26, 1957, to inform Tulie Ferrier that the United States Government had recognized John Ferrier's final act of courage by awarding him, posthumously, the Distinguished Flying Cross.

The Denver Post, in an editorial entitled "The Highest Brand of Heroism," said, "The manner of Capt. John T. Ferrier's dying deserves a salute of deepest respect," and noted that Ferrier "sacrificed his life to save a possible score of others."

"It was," said the Post, "the kind of heroism that keeps the fine traditions of our fighting forces fresh."

Shorty thereafter, the people of Davenport, Iowa, where the Minute Men had performed several times, established a "John Ferrier Trophy," which is presented at the city's annual Air Fair to the outstanding Boy Scout of the area.

This fall, as Ferrier's fellow pilots of the Colorado Air National Guard return to active duty to insure the defense of their country, the people of Colorado can again remember Capt. John T. Ferrier.

As one Air Guard officer commented, "An American poet, Sam Foss once wrote, 'Bring me men to match my mountains.' Well, Ferrier was one of those men...

We don't have to fear any enemy as long as America can produce people of the stature of John Ferrier."

Ferrier Scholarship at Kanakuk

John Arnette
(Kanakuk Kamp: 1948-1961)

Hi, Darnell! After 13 years at Kanakuk (that would be a total of about two years if you count the 2 months each summer x's 13 years = 26 months) I would certainly have a few tales about Kamp!

The first year I came to Kanakuk was 1949. That year was the same year my aunt and uncle took my sister, Joyce, and me into their home as our guardians. I lived with them until I graduated from college. I can remember my first year because I had never been away from home, and my mother had to give us up to her sister, Aunt Thera, and my Uncle DeVan Sharbrough. Boy was I ever "homesick!" I was in Cabin 1 and my counselors were Ray Cravens and Jim Welch. I would cry every night. To help me out and not make other Kampers "homesick" and lose sleep, Ray Cravens put up a tent with a couple of sleeping bags just outside the Cabin (next to the Toothbrush Check-in Stand). Ray and Jim would alternate sleeping with me in the tent. I had several nights of that until all the activities kept me busy, then I wanted to be back in Cabin One with the other kids. Reflecting back on that first act of kindness, understanding, and compassion, truly it was the Spirit of Kanakuk that made me grow up!

One of the Sports events at Kanakuk happened to me and stayed with me all the way through college. Early on when I was a Kamper, Johnny Rutherford, a counselor, picked me to be a pole vaulter. (I don't know why he chose me except maybe he knew I wasn't afraid of anything and would try anything at least once.) Johnny took me down to the track and held a steel pole, told me to go back down the runway, run, and grab the pole where he threw me over the bar while hanging on to the pole. In those days, all Kamp had was a flat sand pit, and I landed IN the pit and rolled OUT.....tumbling everywhere. He worked with me for hours. Each summer, Johnny was there at Kamp and coached me. In 1959, the lower track flooded just before the Final Track Meet, and a new track was hastily built up on the Baseball Field area near the Council Ring. The Pole Vault Record was one of the oldest records still standing at Kanakuk, and that year I broke the record! The Pole Vault earned me my first "K" Letter in Track and Field and later a scholarship to college, all because one counselor saw something in a small boy. That boy came within a little over one foot off the World Record that Dutch Warmerdamm held for many years (he used a bamboo pole). I am reminded many times of the memories from all my Meets of that one man who "picked me out" and believed in me. The training was also instrumental in my excelling in College Swimming/Diving and Gymnastics that I first learned in Kamp.

The Pole Vault earned me my first "K" Letter in Track and Field and later a scholarship to College, all because one Counselor saw something in a small boy.

One of the years when I was in the Senior Division, Boxing Night was scheduled, and the Cherokees had a big ole' boy to fight, and the Choctaws couldn't get any of our guys to volunteer to take him on. My Tribe "buddies" chanted "Let John fight him! John's not afraid of anyone." Well, I got creamed, but was still left alive. After the pummeling, Spike felt sorry for me and took me down to the kitchen to serve me two bowls full of homemade peppermint ice cream that the kitchen girls had just made. (I should have put some on my swollen eyes and fat lip!)

Thinking about food and the Dining Hall Waitresses from the School of The Ozarks, those were some of the greatest times of real joy. I think I still have nicks in my elbow from guys catching me with my "elbows on the table."

Here again, I don't know why I was chosen, but Spike came to me one day and asked if I wanted to learn how to do some of the Indian dances at the Campfire Ceremonies. Spike, Nocus McIntosh and I danced together, and it was a great honor for me. My favorite dance was the Hoop Dance. I was small in size and could easily get through the Hoop, but I was amazed at how agile and muscular Spike was at dancing the Hoop Dance with THREE hoops! I loved the entrance when we "Indians" would quietly creep out of the dark woods until arriving at the Circle of Kampers at Ring of Fire and start yelling like Indians on a War Path, and jumping "over" the Kampers and dancing as we landed.

One of the hardest and best years I had at Kamp was in 1958 when I was Choctaw Chief. Competition was great, but the relationships that were made for me as Chief are unforgettable. I got to know the youngest tribal members in Cabin One to the Senior Division Choctaws in Cabin Twelve. At that time, the oldest boys in Cabin 12 had no Counselors. (The famous Cabin Twelve Trail probably holds stories that need not be published!) That year, as Chief, I was privileged to serve meals to Uncle Bob at his Cabin and got to know him much better. Many years I was at Kamp and thought he was a ghost (like the "Slough Lady"). Although we could see the work that he and Spike did, we rarely saw Uncle Bob. When I became Chief and visited with him when I took meals to him, I thought that was pretty neat.

Also, 1958 was the year that Kanakomo Kamp for Girls started. I recall one afternoon when the boys were Water Skiing, I asked the Boat Driver to run me by the girls' dock (of course, to "show off"). As we approached, I thought I could get close enough to make a sharp turn and spray the girls, but, as usual, I was not paying attention. The low diving board was sticking out, and I just caught a glimpse of it and let go of the rope in time to go under the board and almost decapitate myself. I had tumbled under water and swallowed water up my nose and throat. I was struggling for air. Girls had to pull me out, and it seemed forever for the boat driver to return to pick me up. Added to that embarrassing and prideful event, I had torn my swim trunks on the dock. I just don't know what gets into guys when girls are around!

Tears of joy and sadness, but mainly of joy for wonderful gift God gave me. . . bringing Kanakuk Kamp and the Whites into my life. Much later I returned to Spike's and Darnell's house and had lunch with Spike. Yes, he made our favorite "PB&Js."

The greatest memory I have of Kanakuk was a sentimental trip to Kamp around year 2000. Since I never knew my own dad, I had grown to feel that Spike was a father to me, and his family was my family. (I am sure hundreds or thousands have felt the same way about the Whites and the Kanakuk family.) I had dropped in Darnell's office and she invited me to visit with Spike at their home by the Council Rink. Spike and I talked about old times, and then he drove me around Kanakuk Kamp in his red pick-up. I was hanging on for dear life, especially when we went down the side of the hill on the narrow and steep dirt road to the bottom by the lake. I thought I was going to bail out a couple of times, but as many times as Spike had driven this road, surely he probably could drive it in his sleep!. . . and I thought that was happening then! Spike pointed out all the new and exciting innovations built since my days as a Kamper. Returning to the top, we walked to the Dining Hall that was named for John Benien. Outside the Dining Hall, Spike pointed out the Record Boards and Chiefs' Names displayed for all to see and reminisce. Spike had kindred feelings, I'm certain, and asked if I would like to get out and walk around by myself and later come to his house and join him for lunch. I walked all over the Kamp that day, and I can hardly sit here and type out the emotions I had for every foot of hallowed ground I covered. The memories were a mix of joy and tears as I walked around Kamp. Remembering the fun times of putting on plays at Taneycomo Court, the Sunday Services at the Outside Church overlooking the Ozark Hills and Lake below where I sat and heard Bill Lantz and Spike deliver the "I'M THIRD' message, to the chinning bar where I had left a pound of flesh trying to win the chinning competition for my Tribe to learning skills that would take me to College Gymnastics Team, to the teeth-cleaning line where we would try to get through without brushing. . . no way! That one day of "looking back" covered the gamut! I even sought out Choctaw Meeting Place. It is hard for me to write this because it is hard to see the monitor through the tears. Tears of joy and sadness, but mainly of joy for a wonderful gift God gave me. . . bringing Kanakuk Kamp and the Whites into my life. Much later I returned to Spike and Darnell's house and had lunch with Spike. Yes, he made our favorite "PB&Js." As I was leaving, riding my motorcycle, and waving "goodbye," I was blinded by tears and nearly crashed into a tree. Down the lane and out-of-sight, I gave way to my emotions and simply cried before departing.

Spike's spirit had been passed on to Joe long ago, and the Spirit of Kanakuk still lives through you, Darnell, and your wonderful son, Joe. The Kanakuk Spirit is the people: C. L. Ford, Ed Walker, Bill Lantz, Spike and Darnell, and now Joe and Debbie Jo. You raised one of the greatest Evangelists of our times: Joe White. It is not just his leadership that has enlarged Kanakuk, but it is also his ability to win souls for Christ. From the many books he has written, to Promise Keepers, the Youth and College Tours, as well as the Inner-City Kamps started and now expanding and serving. The list goes on and on.

God bless you and all your families.
I love you as a son,
John

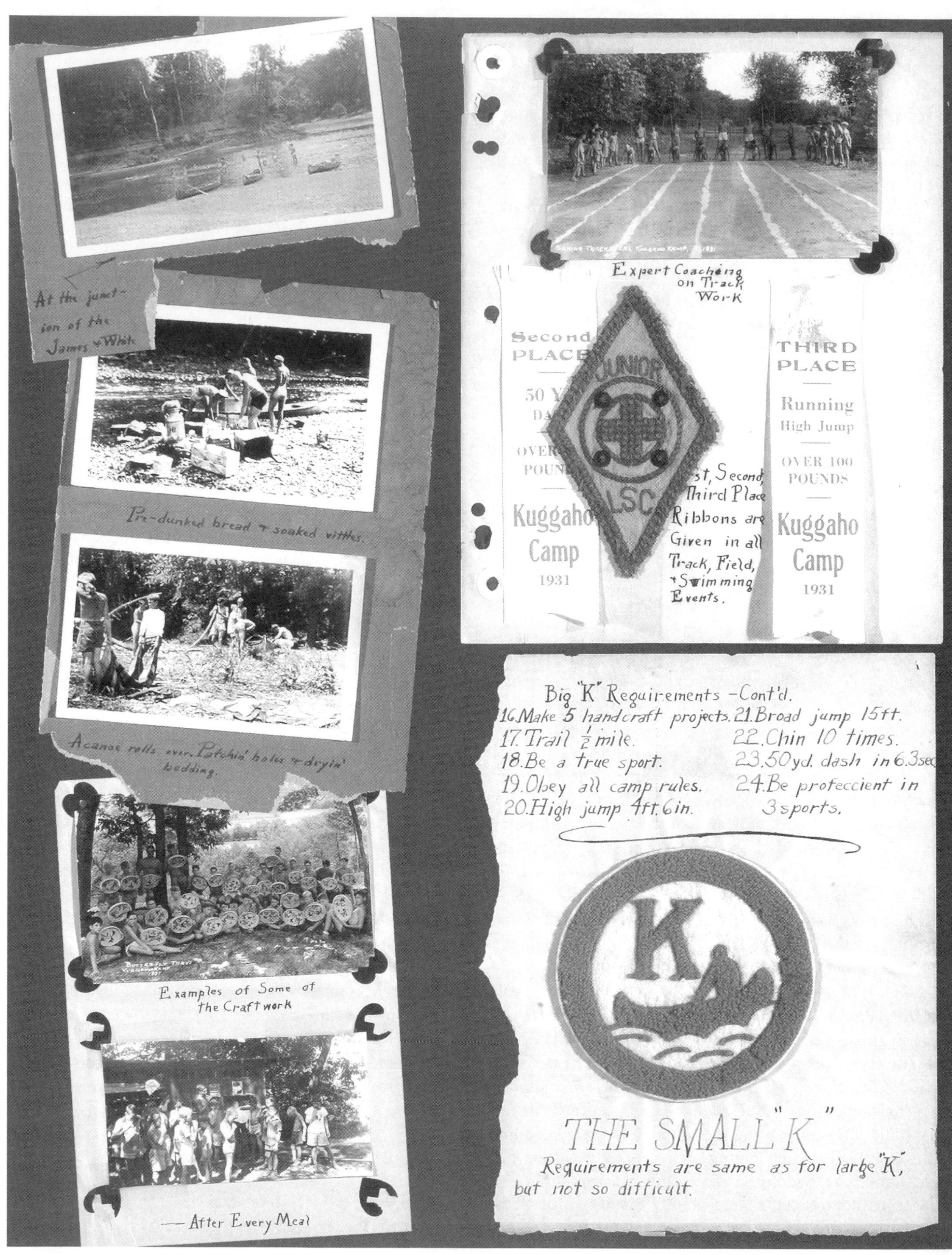
At the junction of the James + White
Pre-dunked bread + soaked vittles.
A canoe rolls over. Patchin' holes + dryin' bedding.
Examples of Some of the Craftwork
— After Every Meal
Expert Coaching on Track Work
Second PLACE
JUNIOR
LSC
Kuggaho Camp
1931
1st, Second, Third Place Ribbons are Given in all Track, Field, + Swimming Events.
THIRD PLACE
Running High Jump
OVER 100 POUNDS
Kuggaho Camp
1931
Big "K" Requirements - Cont'd.
16. Make 5 handcraft projects.
17. Trail 1/2 mile.
18. Be a true sport.
19. Obey all camp rules.
20. High jump 4ft. 6in.
21. Broad jump 15ft.
22. Chin 10 times.
23. 50yd. dash in 6.3sec
24. Be profeccient in 3 sports.
K
THE SMALL "K"
Requirements are same as for large "K", but not so difficult.

THE BIG "K"

Requirements—

1. Hike 75 miles.
2. Handle canoe well.
3. Handle horse well.
4. Shoot 35 out of possible 50 with rifle.
5. Equivalent in archery.
6. Swim lake + back.
7. Pass Jr. Red Cross L.S.
8. Know 10 birds.
9. Know 10 trees
10. Know constellations.
11. Know poison ivy.
12. Know characteristics of poisonous snakes.
13. Tie 5 knots.
14. Pass first aid.
15. Catch, mount, + identify 5 kinds butterflies.

(over)

Excerpts of "Spike's"

1931 KAMP SCRAPBOOK

Made by "Spike" White, a 17 year-old Junior Counselor

What To Bring To Camp

2 pair of blankets
1 pillow
4 sheets
2 pillow cases
1 sweater
Tennis shoes
8 bath towels
2 bathing suits
1 pair overalls
~~2 pair white knickers~~ 2 Pair Long White
~~2 pair white golf socks,~~ Pants
2 white shirts
4 pair "shorts"
Rain coat or poncho
Flash light
~~Sailor hat~~
~~1 black~~ four-in-hand tie black Tie

We want the boys to feel free to dress almost as they please and hence we are not prescribing any set uniform except for Sundays. We expect every boy to be dressed in white on Sunday with a black four-in-hand tie.

Baseball equipment, tennis rackets, tennis balls, musical instruments, fishing tackle, kodaks, ~~hammocks, and character costumes for stunts and plays should be brought to camp if possible.~~

Bedding should be packed in heavy duck bags and sent express prepaid or by parcel post to the owners address in care of KUGGAHO KAMP, Branson, Mo., at least a week before camp opens. Trunks should be checked two days before leaving if possible.

Very Little Equipment Is Needed

The cost in each camp is $250, which includes a dollar each week for laundry and all other necessary expenses except Railroad fare. <u>There are no extras for any camp activities.</u>

All railroads have excursion rates to the OZARKS. The round trip rate from Dallas is $21.70, $31.50 from Amarillo.

Branson Bridge over Taney...

The kitchen canoe runs aground & rolls over. →

We Stop For A Swim.

At Bull Creek

An Overnight Trip

TRIBAL COMPETITION, KUGGAHO KAMP 1931

CHEROKEES KUGGAHO KAMP 1931

Cherokees

This years winning tribe.

The Toothbrush Charts and Final Ceremony

This is a story worthy of repeating. It all happened the last night of the term after TAPS had sounded and the Kampers at the boys' Kamp were in bed. The Directors and Staff were meeting in the Dining Hall to prepare for the Final Ceremony where all KAMP, parents, and visitors attended in anticipation of the Winning Tribe announcement, and individual Awards Presentation: "K"s," Ribbons for Sport Events, Honor Kamper, Trip Paddles, and I'm Third. The meeting the night before was important. Totals of points won on the Charts were compiled for the everyday competition in sports played between the Tribes: the Final Track Meet and Swimming Meet results, Individual Tribal Champions for other Games (Ping Pong, Checkers, Washers, Wrestling, Horse Shoes, and Tribal Stunts (plays presented at Taneycomo Court), all are entered in the Book to be announced for the Final Ceremony. This particular night the total for all points accumulated during the summer was totaled several times, and the numbers were tied! Most times the difference in points does not necessitate the tiresome and important totaling of the of the Toothbrush Charts. That summer the Toothbrush Charts were of major importance.

Toothbrush Charts are made in columns with three daily entries, one for each Kamper times the number of days in the Term. It is required for every Kamper to brush his teeth after each meal. After he has brushed, he steps in the line to get a "check" registered by his Chief (lots of "checks" to be totaled for each of the two TRIBES). In the wee hours of the night, the relieved and weary Staff agree on the points and arrive at the FINAL COUNT of the Winner of the TRIBE that won.

After breakfast the last day of each Term, Kampers, parents, visitors, and Staff meet at the foot of the Flag Pole to hear the announcement of the Winning Tribe for that year. The Chiefs stand together and the waiting is filled with excitement and anxiety. After the winner is announced, the loud yelling of either joy and relief of the Winning Tribe or the moans and disappointments of the Losing Tribe calms down, the two Chiefs (or Princesses at the Girls' Kamp Ceremony) read the WILL they have written together to leave for the Chiefs and Tribal members next summer. A Peace Pipe is passed from one Chief to the other and then the Peace Pipe, the Will, and the War Hatchet are buried in the chest and covered with soil-not to be opened again until the next year.

NATIONAL RIFLE ASSOCIATION
JUNIOR
DIPLOMA
THIS IS TO CERTIFY THAT
DAN SCOTT
HAS QUALIFIED AS
Marksman
having made a score of twenty-five points or better, out of a possible fifty points on each of ten official N.R.A. fifty foot targets.
In testimony thereof, this diploma is given at our hands this 16th day of August in the year of 1937
National Rifle Association
Washington, D.C.
Ed Reynolds
INSTRUCTOR
DIRECTOR OF JUNIOR
FIRST PLACE
DIVING
JUNIOR
Kanakuk Kamp
1937
FIRST PLACE
SWIMMING
50 YD. Back Stroke
SENIOR
Kanakuk Kamp
1941
FIRST PLACE
TRACK
FOOTBALL THROW
SENIOR
Kanakuk Kamp
1941
NATURE STUDY AWARD
Kanakuk Kamp
1935
WOODWORK AWARD
Kanakuk Kamp
1935
JUNIOR
DIPLOMA
THIS IS TO CERTIFY THAT
Dan Scott
HAS QUALIFIED AS
Marksman-First Class
having made a score of thirty points or better, out of a possible fifty points on each of ten official N.R.A. fifty foot targets. In testimony
this diploma is given at our hands this 21st day of August
year of 1942
National Rifle Association
Washington, D.C.
W.E. Hagan
INSTRUCTOR
C.B. Lister
SECRETARY-TREASURER
FIRST PLACE
TRACK
100 YD. Dash
JUNIOR
Kanakuk Kamp
1938
NATIONAL RIFLE ASSOCIATION
JUNIOR
DIPLOMA
THIS IS TO CERTIFY THAT
Dan Scott
HAS QUALIFIED AS A
Pro-Marksman
having made a score of twenty points or better, out of a possible fifty points on each of ten official N.R.A. fifty foot targets. In Testimony thereof, this Diploma is given at our hands this 27th day of August in the year of 1935
National Rifle Association
Washington, D.C.
MANAGER
JUNIOR DIVISION
FIRST PLACE
TRACK
FOOTBALL THROW
SENIOR
Kanakuk Kamp
1942
TENNIS CHAMPION
JUNIOR
Kanakuk Kamp
1937
FIRST PLACE
TRACK
DISCUS
SENIOR
Kanakuk Kamp
1942
SECOND PLACE
TRACK
50 YD. Dash
JUNIOR
Kanakuk Kamp
1938

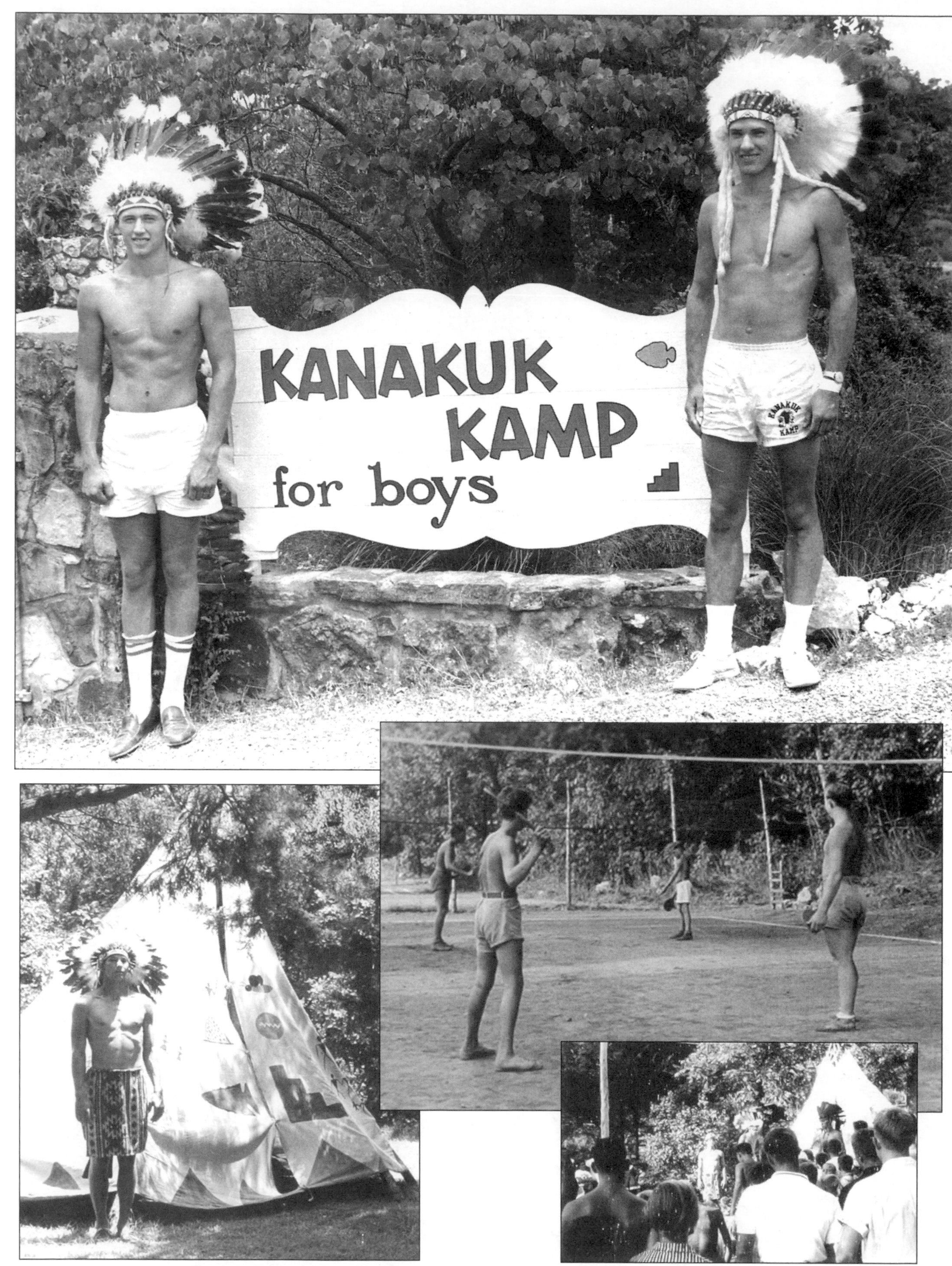
KANAKUK
KAMP
for boys

Opening Ceremony (The following year)

The second day of the Term the following year, the Kamp Director or Head Honcho calls out each first-time Kamper by name and announces the Tribe he belongs to, and the Kamper gathers with his Tribe. The two new Chiefs, who are standing at the Flag Pole on top of the Fountain stage, unbury the Will, the Peace Pipe, and the Hatchet. The Chiefs read the Will that was written to this year's Chiefs and their Tribes. The Hatchet is then held high, indicating that War is declared between the two Tribes until the end of the Term.
"LET THE COMPETITION BEGIN!"

Clips from Chinnubbie McIntosh

It is only when we take time to pause and reflect on the past that we realize the early years were truly character forming years. Bill Lantz taught me how to lose. Between Bill and my Dad, I learned defeat is not a word to believe in. There are only moments in life with temporary set-backs. Bill taught his Track team members to live, not hibernate! Track and Kanakuk discipline kept me in good stead. Indian language there is a cry of "Mahe" (pronounced "Maw-Hey"). It is a word called by the women dancers to get the men dancers to join them in the ring. It is a beautiful word with a beautiful meaning. I feel it applied to Coach Lantz: "Here he comes... TALL."

I was 15 years of age, painfully shy and somewhat scared, having just moved from a small town when I entered Tulsa Central High School. It was in gym class that I first met Coach Bill Lantz. He was somewhat short in height, but had a physical and spiritual quality that everyone just wanted to be around. Since I was too small to go the football or basketball route, track was to be my sport. This meant a transfer to Coach Lantz's 6th hour class, where all the athletes were. The older boys informed me that to get in 6th hour, the last class of the day, there were two requirements: a crew cut (in the army called a "GI"), and a belt.

Our family's move to Tulsa and training for Track under Bill Lantz (with my Dad's influence) was the beginning of the development of staunch attributes, discipline, and teachings of Bill's leadership. In gym class, Bill demonstrated on the equipment. He performed on the pommel horse and explained that it takes years to build up the wrists to do the movements. He had magnificent wrist and forearm muscles. How fortunate I was to get double dose of Coach Lantz at school and later at Kanakuk Kamp. Coach Lantz invited me to be a Junior Counselor at Kanakuk Kamp. Summers spent at Kamp and the other nine months on Coach's Track Team formed the rest of my life's direction.

He spoke of his youth in Nebraska: of ice skating up to 90 miles a day from one lake to another, by holding up his jacket over his head, thereby creating a small sail. Another time he mentioned doing the high diving act on the high platform, up to 100', similar to the acts in the traveling Carnivals. He told of challenging the wrestlers in the Carnival side shows to win money to take his school wrestling teams on trip competitions. He told of wrestling a world champion in his weight class to a four-hour draw.

Many times he was called "Ace" because of his air-flying ability. One time in gym class, Bill put a pair of coconut halves on his hands, and standing on his hands

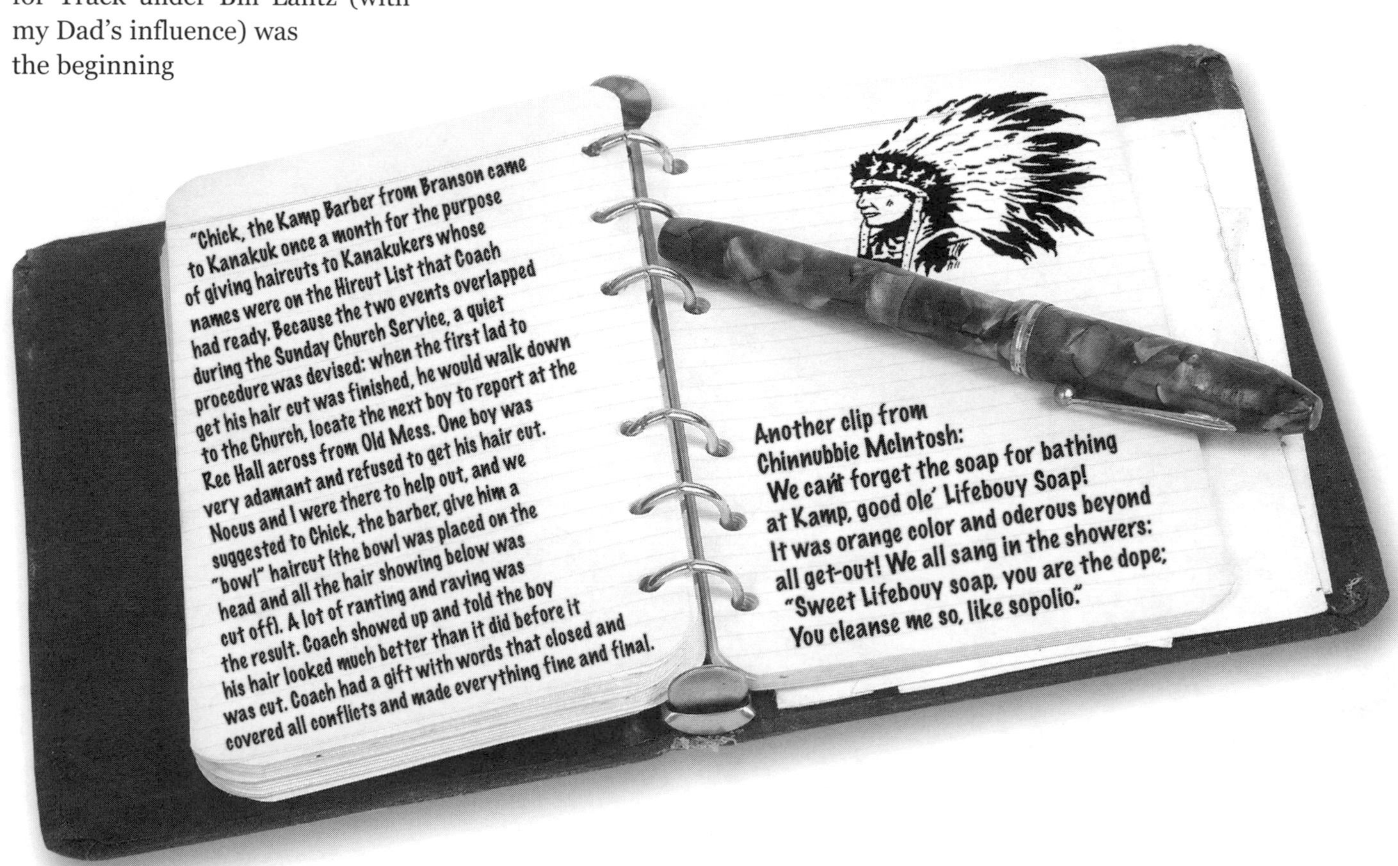

"Chick, the Kamp Barber from Branson came
to Kanakuk once a month for the purpose
of giving haircuts to Kanakukers whose
names were on the Hircut List that Coach
had ready. Because the two events overlapped
during the Sunday Church Service, a quiet
procedure was devised: when the first lad to
get his hair cut was finished, he would walk down
to the Church, locate the next boy to report at the
Rec Hall across from Old Mess. One boy was
very adamant and refused to get his hair cut.
Nocus and I were there to help out, and we
suggested to Chick, the barber, give him a
"bowl" haircut (the bowl was placed on the
head and all the hair showing below was
cut off). A lot of ranting and raving was
the result. Coach showed up and told the boy
his hair looked much better than it did before it
was cut. Coach had a gift with words that closed and
covered all conflicts and made everything fine and final.
Another clip from
Chinnubbie McIntosh:
We can't forget the soap for bathing
at Kamp, good ole' Lifebouy Soap!
It was orange color and oderous beyond
all get-out! We all sang in the showers:
"Sweet Lifebouy soap, you are the dope;
You cleanse me so, like sopolio."

tapped out a rhythm. The two halves had a strap over the cone top.

Bill Lantz was such a great listener. He always had a glint in his eye. It reflected humor, friendship, mischief and love for his fellow man. The Track Team, every Friday, ran a 1.5 mile course around the park and cemetary east of school. Bill ran with us. One time he hollered, "Look out, Chinnubbie" and shoved me to where I had to run down a slanted hillside and catch back up. Talk about a man of mischief!

Coach Lantz's Cross Country Teams won the State Run every year. He was installed in the Sports Hall of Fame in Oklahoma.

Coach Lantz always found some weeds that needed cutting, that had a sly message about counselors who stayed out too late on their "nights off" and for other misdemeanors that needed to be accounted for. The next day during the Rest Period after lunch (best part of the day), Coach had "weeds in some field, sun shining down hot, that needed cutting."

— another "Chinnubbie" memory

The "Blobs" that Kampers play on at the Kamps today are a far cry from the ones Nucus and I installed in the 1940's. When Nocus and I proudly took to Kamp our sleeping bags and life rafts that we bought from an Army Surplus Store, "King of the Mountain" The kids loved it, especially knocking each other off the raft into the cold water.

Chinnubbie story: "There was the "Ice-cream Maker" kept in the corner of "Ole' Mess" and turned by hand. Carl Jackson and "Snake" Jacobs took turns turning the handle, adding the rock salt to the brine, etc. As the cream thickened, it had to be eaten down to keep the lid on. No wonder they volunteered for the job! "Snake" held the record of eating 21 dips and was sick the rest of the day. That ended their "ice cream-making" career. Once a week, all-Kamp got one or two dips with the noon meal. The leftovers went to the winners of the Stunt Night at the next meal.

Betty Rutherford and Nell Lantz stayed in the Rock House all day, except when they would go into town on errands. Two boys received a discount on Kamp admission fee for taking food trays to the rock house, which was a short path across from the Mess Hall, to the ladies at mealtimes.

Submitted by Chinnubbie

Since we had 8 weeks in the early days, we got to know one another pretty well. Therefore some were known by "nick names" which they were fondly called. Some of these names stuck with them forever. Here are a few that I can recall:

Hoss Fly
Pear
Bull Frog
Tally Ho Tally
Chinni
Roaring Weaver
Wagal Woman
Bartley
Bean Pole
Oriental Gong

Sparrow
Motor Mouth
D-Vote
Puppy Dog
Big Earl
Tommy Tucker
Gillissippi
and, oh yes, there was
Bird Legs and
McKinan

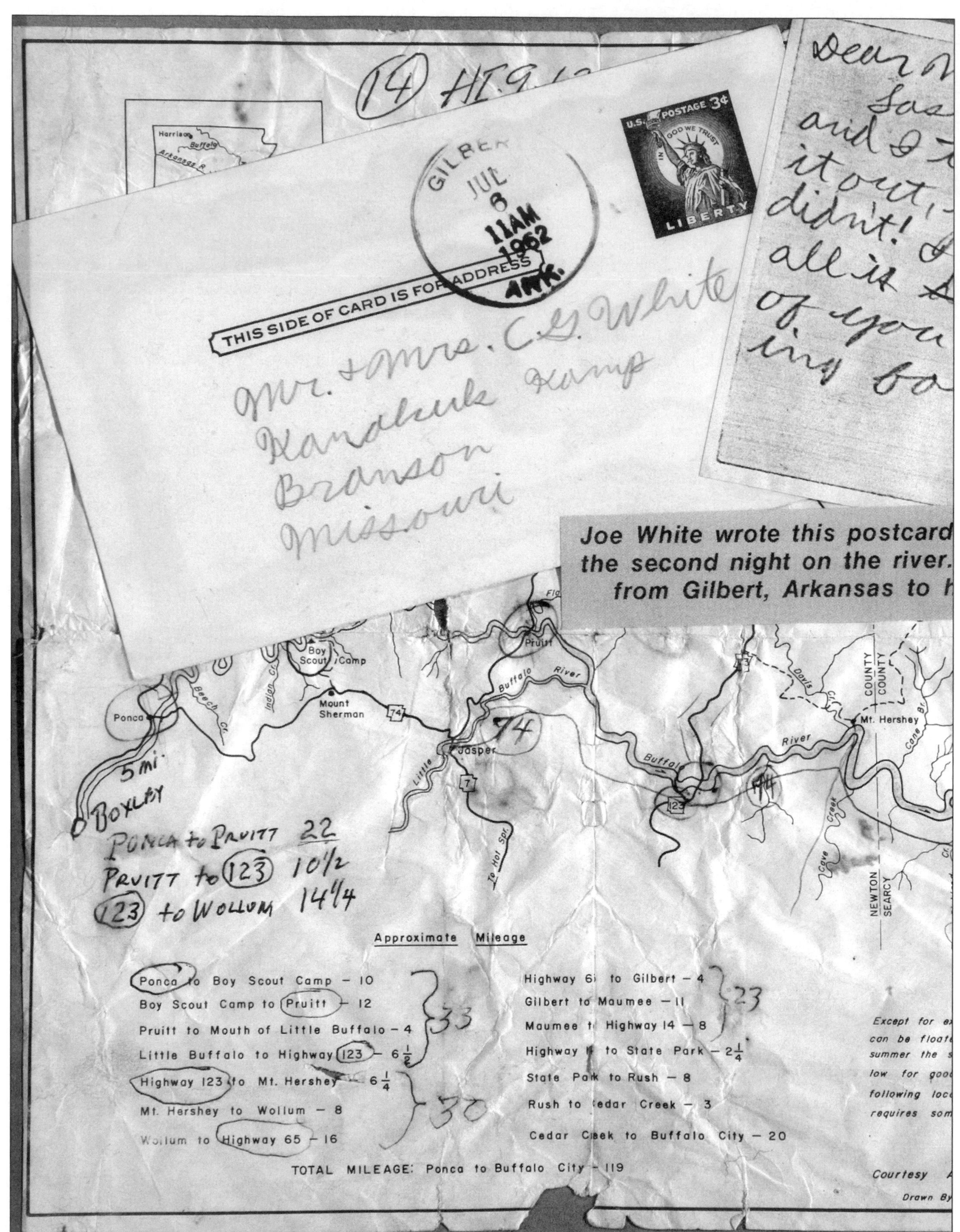

U.S. POSTAGE 3¢
IN GOD WE TRUST
LIBERTY
GILBERT
JUL 3
11 AM
1962
ARK.
THIS SIDE OF CARD IS FOR ADDRESS
Mr. & Mrs. C.G. White
Branson
Missouri
Joe White wrote this postcard
the second night on the river.
from Gilbert, Arkansas to h
Harrison
Buffalo
Arkansas R.
Boy Scout Camp
Ponca
Beech Cr.
Indian Cr.
Mount Sherman
Pruitt
Buffalo River
Jasper
Little
To Hot Spr.
Davis Cr.
Mt. Hershey
River
Buffalo
Cane Br.
Cave Creek
NEWTON COUNTY
SEARCY COUNTY
5 mi.
Boxley
Ponca to Pruitt 22
Pruitt to 123 10½
123 to Wollum 14¼
Approximate Mileage
Ponca to Boy Scout Camp – 10
Boy Scout Camp to Pruitt – 12
Pruitt to Mouth of Little Buffalo – 4
Little Buffalo to Highway 123 – 6½
Highway 123 to Mt. Hershey – 6¼
Mt. Hershey to Wollum – 8
Wollum to Highway 65 – 16
33
30
Highway 65 to Gilbert – 4
Gilbert to Maumee – 11
Maumee to Highway 14 – 8
Highway 14 to State Park – 2¼
State Park to Rush – 8
Rush to Cedar Creek – 3
Cedar Creek to Buffalo City – 20
23
TOTAL MILEAGE: Ponca to Buffalo City – 119
Courtesy
Drawn By

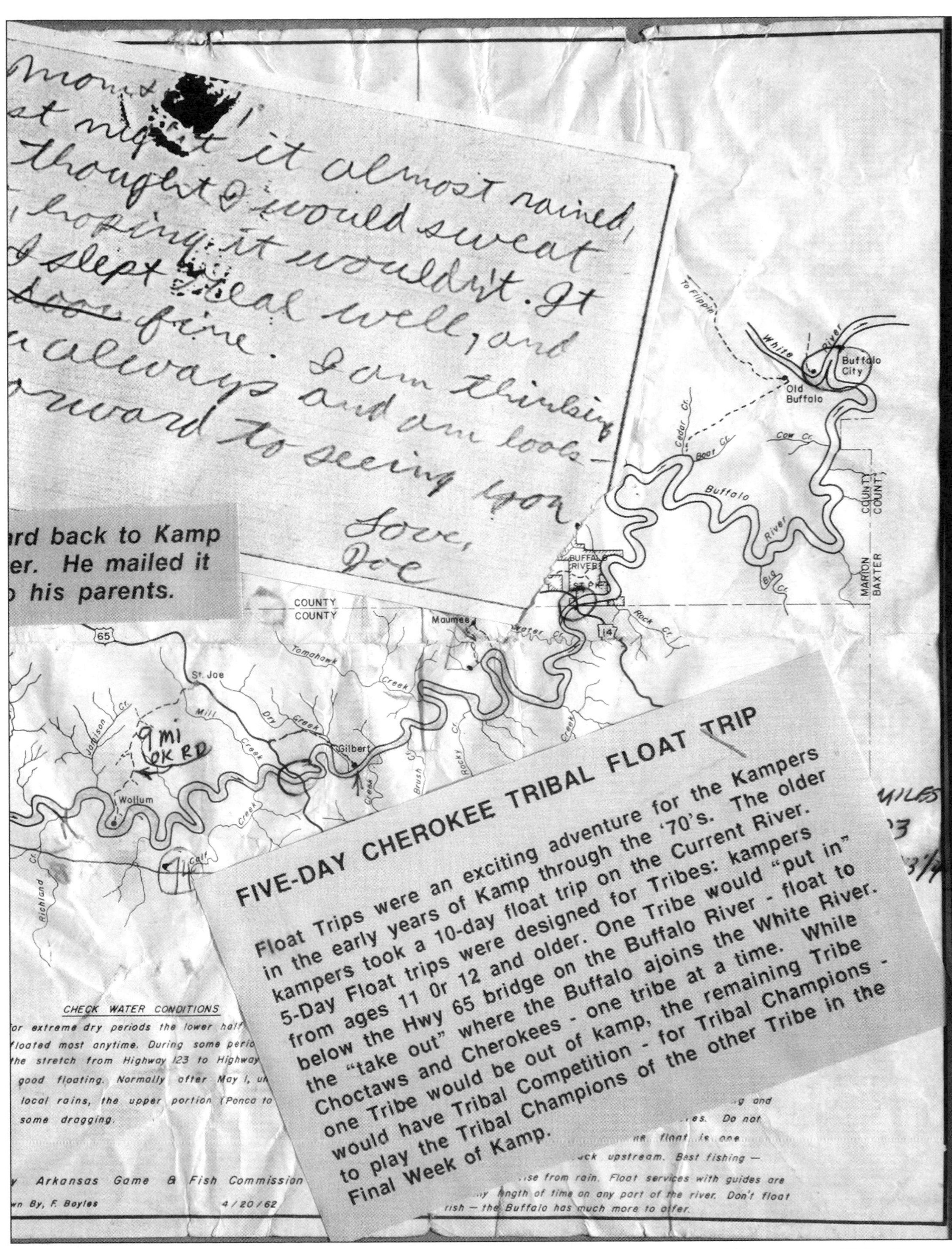

FIVE-DAY CHEROKEE TRIBAL FLOAT TRIP

Float Trips were an exciting adventure for the Kampers in the early years of Kamp through the '70's. The older kampers took a 10-day float trip on the Current River. 5-Day Float trips were designed for Tribes: kampers from ages 11 Or 12 and older. One Tribe would "put in" below the Hwy 65 bridge on the Buffalo River - float to the "take out" where the Buffalo ajoins the White River. Choctaws and Cherokees - one tribe at a time. While one Tribe would be out of kamp, the remaining Tribe would have Tribal Competition - for Tribal Champions - to play the Tribal Champions of the other Tribe in the Final Week of Kamp.

Float Trips

Dick Baldwin shared a few thoughts on the float trips he had at Kanakuk Kamp: "For whatever reason, food was always better cooked outdoors on a float trip." He described an initiation ritual for float trips was getting caught walking barefoot on a gravel bar: a buddy would show up on each side of you for a brief run! Fishing was always possible unless you were Sam Bradshaw's canoe partner; then your job was to put the canoe in just the correct spot for Sam to cast his fly-rod."

That reminded me of a canoe trip that Spike told about. In 1931, Spike sold magazines in order to make enough money to buy an advertised rod and reel that he wanted very much. He met the requirements in time to bring it to Kanakuk the following summer. He and his buddy Loris Moody were canoe partners on the trip. Spike was proud of his rod and reel until the canoe swamped in the middle of an unexpected white water rapid. While hastily retrieving from the fast-sweeping river the food that had been packed in their canoe, the rod and reel was lost. Early the following morning, Spike persuaded Loris to go back upstream to retreive the rod and reel. They found it!

Dick also shared, "Frog gigging was a late night float trip event. The bright light of the lantern or flashlight gave us the edge because the frogs stayed perfectly still as long as the light was in their eyes. Being patient and persistent was a worthy reward at breakfast the next morning when fried frog legs were served for anyone interested."

Bob White reminded me of float trip for senior-division Kampers. At the near end of the trip, the trippers came down the Buffalo River that met with the White River. They were to paddle up the White River to the designated place where Spike would pick them up. Bob related that the last mile and a half up the fierce flow of the White River was the most challenging any of the trippers had experienced. Each canoe could be seen keeping as close as possible to the sides of the river giving an opportunity to be able to grab a branch of a tree that might be hanging low. The paddlers would try to catch some relief and rest until arriving at the "take out" site.

They were a day early!

With a free afternoon, different excursions and activities were pursued. Nocus McIntosh and Jim Welch, in charge of the trip, decided to explore an area of field a distance away from the Kamp. Across the river was a big cliff that a few boys chose to investigate for possibilities of a cave. Condy Pugh and Bob White were satisfied to fish around the campsite. Long after most of the floaters had been gone, a couple of Kampers came running back from the cliff, screaming that two boys had fallen off the cliff! Bob and Condy, sizing up the conditions, grabbed two cots, crossed the river in two john-boats and climbed the cliff to the victims, Bill Martin and Joe Byrd. Bill had a compound break and Joe Byrd had what turned out to be a broken pelvis. Condy and Bob used the cot sticks and rope to immobilize Bill's leg then secured Joe Byrd, each on the home-remedy-cots-for-gurneys and descended the cliff where a couple of men were fishing. The two fishermen had a small station wagon and drove Bob, Condy, Bill Martin and Joe Byrd to the hospital in Mountain Home, AR. Bill Martin's father flew from Oklahoma to pick up his son and Joe Byrd for more advanced medical attention. The doctor at the

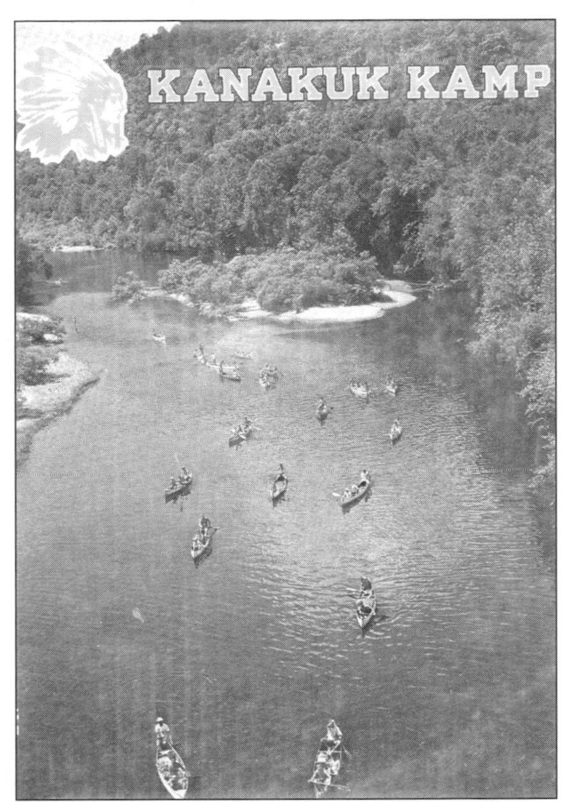

Mountain Home Hospital did not remove the cot sticks and wrap that Condy and Bob had engineered. He said, "That is a fine job and I could not have done better."

Bill and Joe had an excellent recovery and healing. Condy Pugh, incidentally, became a medical doctor in California and favored working in the Emergency Unit. That float trip and the repercussions obviously made an indelible impression on Condy's and Bob's chosen vocations. Bob White became a Pre-Med student at SMU; his vocation became Denistry.

No doubt that every float trip had its own story! Many times when there were long, heavy rainfalls, I recall Spike leaving at 4-5 o'clock in the morning with tons of provisions to check up on the floaters, despite his great confidence in the counselors and the Head Trip man, Rocky Rockhold.

For sure, watermelons growing in open fields, were tempting to a bunch of "city" boys, and this often became cause for "points off" and a serious unbraiding, as well as confrontation and settlement with the farmer whose field was infitrated! (I always dreaded hearing about these raids for fear one of our sons was involved. I knew well that they "took after me in many ways" and not their common-sensed and "do-right" Dad.)

Kamps' float trips stand alone, uniquely making "boys into men." Being away from the conveniences of ice for drinks on hot days, soft mattresses, fans to cool the cabins, clean sheets and clothes, there, on gravel bars, after a meal cooked in the open, feeling full and free, everyone "laid back," wound-down from the activities and adventure of canoeing, no place to go but just "enjoy" sharing the experiences, mesmerized looking into the fire flames, wrapped in the quiet, soft night with sounds of the woods, and the running water not far away. . . these were "special things" a fellow remembers forever.

Many Kampers accepted Christ personally as Jim Welch or some counselor talked and Kampers gave testimonies. It has been verified that the greatest and most meaningful memories are found on the float trips and the camaraderie and rare experiences impacted on their hearts.

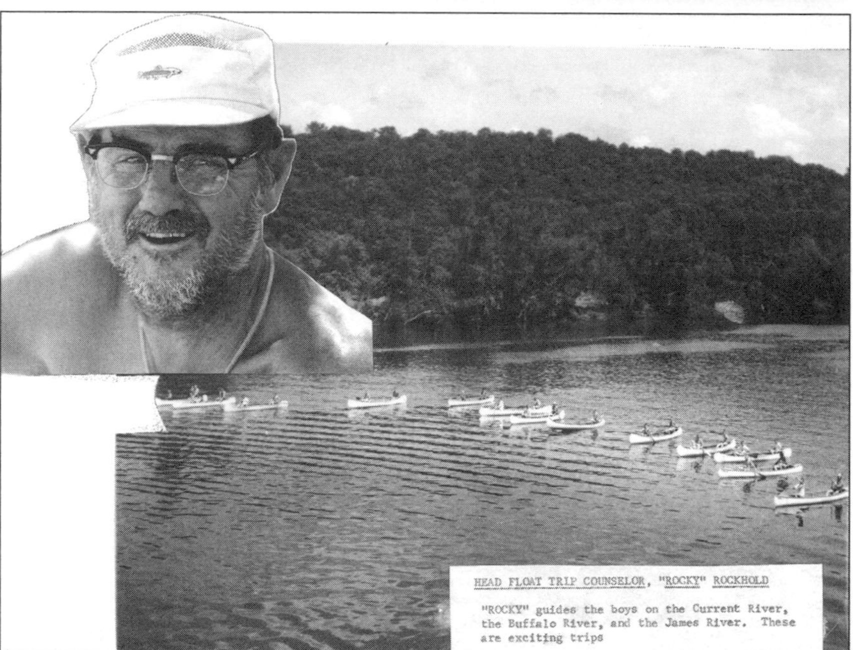

HEAD FLOAT TRIP COUNSELOR, "ROCKY" ROCKHOLD

"ROCKY" guides the boys on the Current River, the Buffalo River, and the James River. These are exciting trips

AN OUTSTANDING STAFF OF CHRISTIAN ATHLETES PROVIDES THE INSPIRATION AND LEADERSHIP SO THAT EACH BOY WILL "INCREASE IN WISDOM, AND STATURE, AND IN FAVOR WITH GOD AND MAN."

Rain on the Float Trip

The anticipation and excitement about special trips out of Kamp grew when there were signs of the special outing shown in front of the Trip Cabin: food being packed, water jugs, grills and cooking utensils being prepared, and heavy camping gear being packed in the Kamp pick up. Years later, canoes Trip Directors, counselors and Kampers increased, a "Trip Girl" from the Dining Hall had the assignment to fill the Provisions List for the Trips. In the old days, Nocus McIntosh would head-up the Trips, and he was in charge of food packing (according to Kamp's menus and foods provided). After Nocus had departed, there would be complaints from the cooks: "cases of Jellies, Juices, Cookies, Peanut Butter missing, and the supplies needed refilling as soon as possible." As I was procurer of foods, it wasn't a great feat to figure out that Nocus had packed the "fun" and easy-to-prepare-stuff everyone preferred for the Trip, in lieu of the Kamp List. How Nocus could manage to re-pack boxes already filled with items for breakfast, lunch and supper and trade off for the "goodies" was a mystery.

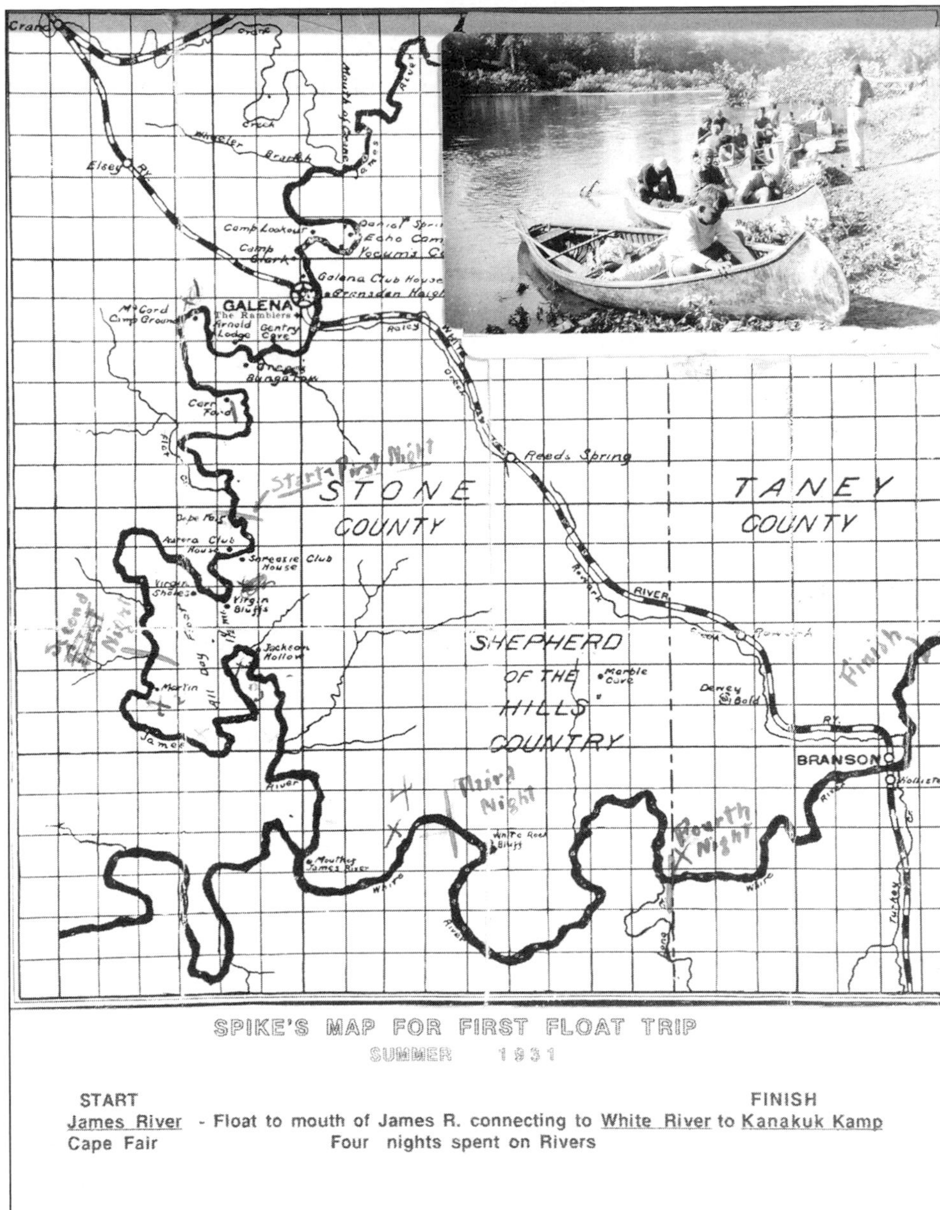

SPIKE'S MAP FOR FIRST FLOAT TRIP
SUMMER 1931

START — James River, Cape Fair - Float to mouth of James R. connecting to White River to Kanakuk Kamp — FINISH
Four nights spent on Rivers

Nocus was popular with the Kampers and Staff; he was a grown-up kid, himself! His energy and enthusiasm were contagious, and everyone was caught up in his joviality and many talents. Before the Girls' Kamp was started, Nocus and his family lived in the Log Cabin that is used for Kanakomo's Infirmary today. Nocus and Jean McIntosh and "Uncle Bob", the groundskeeper, were the only occupants at Kamp during the off-seasons. Nocus was a P.E. teacher at the Branson School nine months of the year. Nocus told great stories of the critters, birds, deer, foxes ("rarely witnessed by most of us") in the fall and winter. Few houses were on this side of the lake, and animals were safe and protected. Winters up until the late '70's were cold with sustained freezes and big snowfalls. One bitter cold winter, Nocus walked down the cliff and across on the frozen Lake going to school.

After Spike, Joe, Debbie Jo and I lived here year 'round, one winter Joe skied from the top of the hill (where the Party Barn is today) down the hill, across Lakeshore Drive, down through Kamp and past the cabin area on to the bottom past Lake Gaddy where the BLOB resides. We all rode sleds from the top of the hill on Lake Shore drive down the bottom of the road north where the long hill flattened out. No traffic! At Christmastime, when all the White Family gathered here, our three sons and their teenage sons played hockey down on the slough. The frozen water would heat up when war was declared 'tween teens and Dads.

Any season Kanakukers get together to play, it is "friendly competition!"

Finding Arrowheads at Kamp

Lennie and Bruce Moss (their sister, Kathy, too) were great Kampers. Their Dad and Mom were unique and it is no wonder why their progeny were special. In fact, Len Moss, the Dad, had been on Staff at one time. He designed, made, and painted the great Gate for the entrance of Kanakuk. It is still the same gate, having been repainted and taken care of all these years.

Lennie Moss was a character out of Huckelberry Finn. Our sons, Bob, Bill, and Joe were close to Lennie's and Bruce's ages, and they always wanted to ride with me when I drove to the Springfield Airport to drive the Moss crew to Kamp. Everyone liked the Mosses, each interesting and special-made. Lennie was a good artist in many forms. He chipped out arrowheads as finely as real Indians. On float trips, many of the Kampers looked for arrowheads because the Indians, some tribes, had settled along the White River. At Kanakuk Kamp our family found some very nice arrowheads. When we came to Kamp early, Spike would take the boys and me to fields that had been furrowed and readied for spring planting. Spring rains washed off a lot of soil, and arrowheads were easier to spot. As we were early arrivals, we would get permission to walk through the fields before they were seeded. We all got excited to look for Indian arrowheads and hand-crafts, no matter if they were whole or just pieces. All would be studied and we would guess at the purpose for the broken flint pieces.

Difficult, really, to know if they were newly made or honest-to-goodness by Indians.

Lennie was crafty and clever and had a good sense of humor. He loved to nonchalantly drop pieces of flint, some broken, some finished into neat arrowheads, enough to excite all the float trippers, when they were discovered. Difficult, really, to know if they were newly made or honest-to-goodness by Indians. In the Kamp movies, Spike showed scenes on the gravel bars with a poncho laid down, and all the treasured arrowheads different Kampers had found displayed. We used to find some fine specimen back in the '50's and '60's! Some of them were made by Lennie Moss. That boy was very, very talented! He had fun being an "elf" who provided his touch of workmanship to make some happy kampers.

Arrowheads

Found On Lakefront of Kanakuk and Trips

As far back as 1350 AD, arrowheads were found in Missouri. Most were darts and spear points, although many were used as knives as well as projectile points. Many times when a projectile point was broken, do to fracture or use, it was made into a knife and crafted into a short wood or bond handle.

There were several "flint-knappers" who made very handsome arrowheads in the likeness of the Indian Tribes that camped on the rivers at one time in the Ozark Hills. All the "pieces" of flint and broken pieces in this picture are original and probably very, very old.

As in places all over the United States where dams have been built and man-made lakes have covered the valleys and river bottom lands where Indians once settled, arrowheads are harder to find today. At the turn of the century and early part of the twentieth century, arrowheads were quite easy to uncover when the spring washed them in the fields, especially when the fields were plowed and prepared for planting.

Fishing Trip on Indian Creek

While I was spending time writing "Patches of The Past" last summer, Bob White often called me from Texas to ask how it was going with the book. I mentioned to him that I had finished a "patch to sew on the KUK quilt" about arrowheads hunted and found down on the track at Kanakuk and on trips out of Kamp. "Mom," he said, "let me tell you about a fishing trip on Indian Creek."

Kanakuk Kamp had several trips for Kampers. Getting to go on any of the trips was exciting. Each trip was distinguished by age groups, Tribal groups and length of days – including Mystery Trips, Truck Trips, and Fishing Trips. Bob was always fired up for "going fishing" (and remains so today).

On a trip to Indian Creek, the Kampers camped on a gravel bar for a couple of days and nights. The counselors and Kampers fished and went on arrowhead hunts in the vicinity where the fields for corn were recently furrowed and planted. It turned out to be more arrowhead-hunting than usual. They had a "field day" - literally! Flints and broken pieces and nearly whole arrowheads and pottery pieces filled their syrup pails along with eye glasses, contact lenses, lip salve, Off for pesky bugs and mosquitoes, sunscreen, toothbrush, and toothpaste. Kamp sold the new galvanized pails with the bails (handles!) for this convenience. Bob remembered that a young boy named David found a beauty of a half-broken arrowhead. David was so proud of that piece and would not quit looking for the other half. In the cool evening on the other side of Indian Creek, someone found the "missing link!" It was uncanny! Everyone rejoiced. The two halves positively "fit together!" A perfect arrowhead.

When Spike picked up the Kampers at Indian Creek, Bob was so excited to tell his dad about David's arrowhead, and he wanted Spike to bring us (Bill, Joe, Bob and me) to hunt together. Spike assured Bob that after Kamp closed and we left to return to Texas, that we would take a few hours to hunt arrowheads at Indian Creek, which we did. The family hunt was not as bountiful as advertised. We had to climb through some prickly shrubs to get to the cornfields which had grown since Kamp's early adventure. It still was a fun outing. Back in the station wagon heading for Texas, all three boys were complaining and moaning as we were traveling south. I leaned over the front seat, and with a flashlight discovered they were covered with seed ticks! I fetched out what little First-Aid we had packed: Campho-phenique, best we had! Not a happy ending, although the boys had found an interesting bowl of Indian nature, making the trip worthwhile.

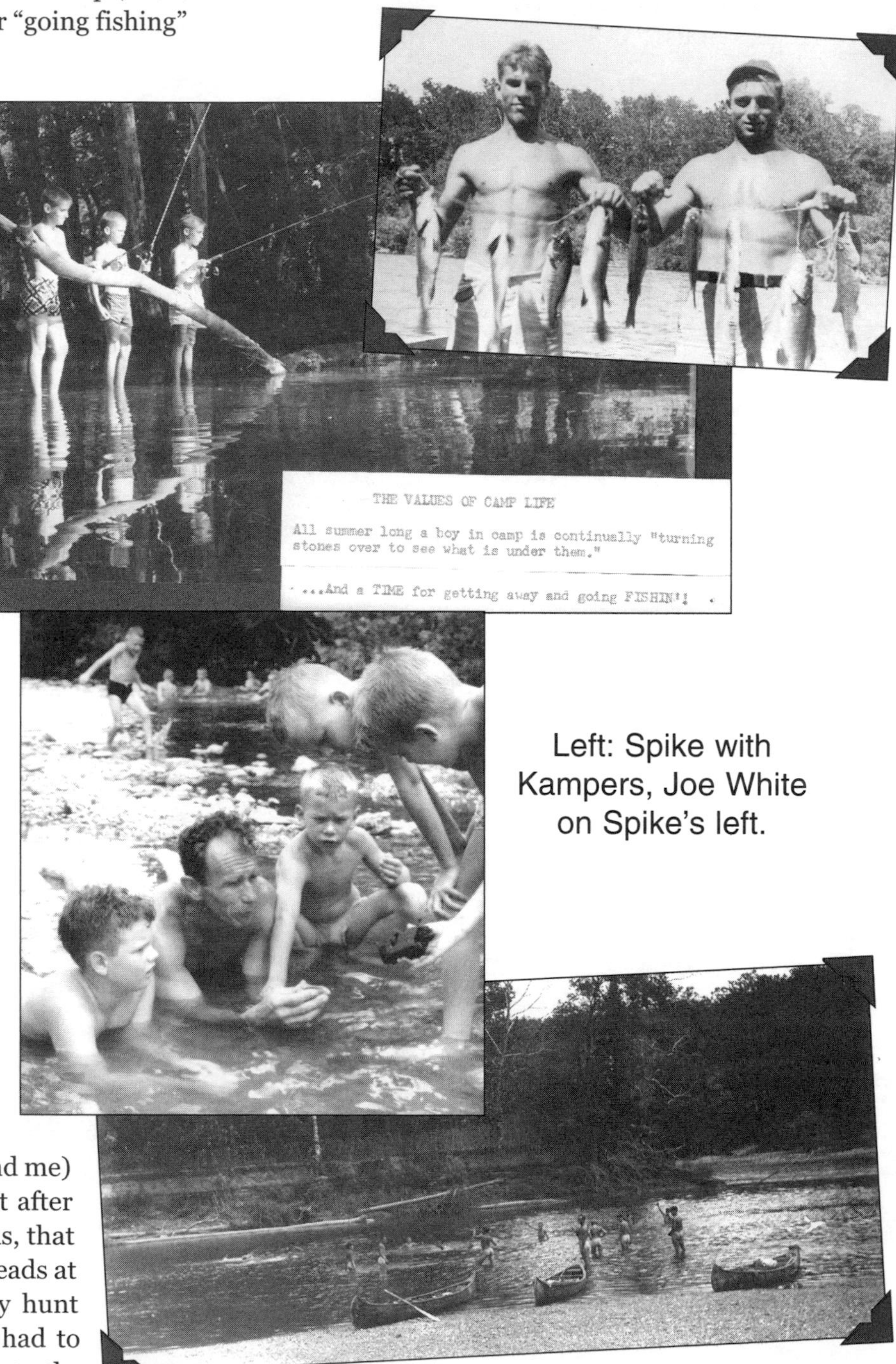

THE VALUES OF CAMP LIFE
All summer long a boy in camp is continually "turning stones over to see what is under them."
...And a TIME for getting away and going FISHIN'!

Left: Spike with Kampers, Joe White on Spike's left.

"Dimies"
Float Trips, Mystery Trips, Truck Trips

There is something special about the trips out of Kamp, and there are lots of stories the Kampers and counselors could tell. I am sure this generation of Kampers has its share of experiences and exciting adventures, also. However, in the '40's, '50's, '60's and '70's, it was another "time" that holds deep in the heart of Kanakuk and Kanakomo Kamps.

Heading back to Kamp after float trips, Spike or who ever drove the bus to the "take-out" on the gravel bar where the trip ended, made a stop at a Dairy Queen, and each Kamper was given one "dimes." That "dimes" represented sheer bliss: it could buy a double-dip, a large cup of ice and Dr. Pepper or Coke! Ice cream cones and iced drinks were manna from heaven to the tired, hot, disheveled float trippers after a 6-or-10-day tripper. They had been on the river floating, swamping, setting up tents at night, and gathering wood for fires for cooking. They had also been eating off of tin plates, been exposed to the mysterious sounds and sights in the dark nightime surroundings, sleeping on the ground in a thin bedroll that might be wet from rain or dunking with a turned-over canoe while floating!

"Dimies" created a lot of planning! Two kampers often saw maximum potential if they combined their "loot" to make "double dimies," and that would buy a drink AND ice cream and two straws! Triple "dimies" was something bigger: Micro economics started in front of a Dairy Queen! It was the essence of "It doesn't get much better than this."

Written by Will Cunningham

Sweet Darnell –

Your recollection of "dimies", though accurate, is slightly less embellished than my own.

Dimies to me were like Leif Erickson's discovery of the new world – so lovely and bountiful that he hardly knew what to do with it. In the end, he sailed away and left its riches for other men to claim.

Darnell, I can't tell you how many times I stood like Leif Erickson at the Dairy Queen counter – money in hand and mouth as wide as a codfish's. I never could articulate my order for lack of air.

Weren't those grand times when thirty cents meant something to a child? Who cared what lay in the holds of Erickson's ship? As long as one had those silver coins in his fat, sweating palm, that was all that mattered.

The counselors called them "triple dimies"... but us kampers called them "a fortune."

Love, Will C.

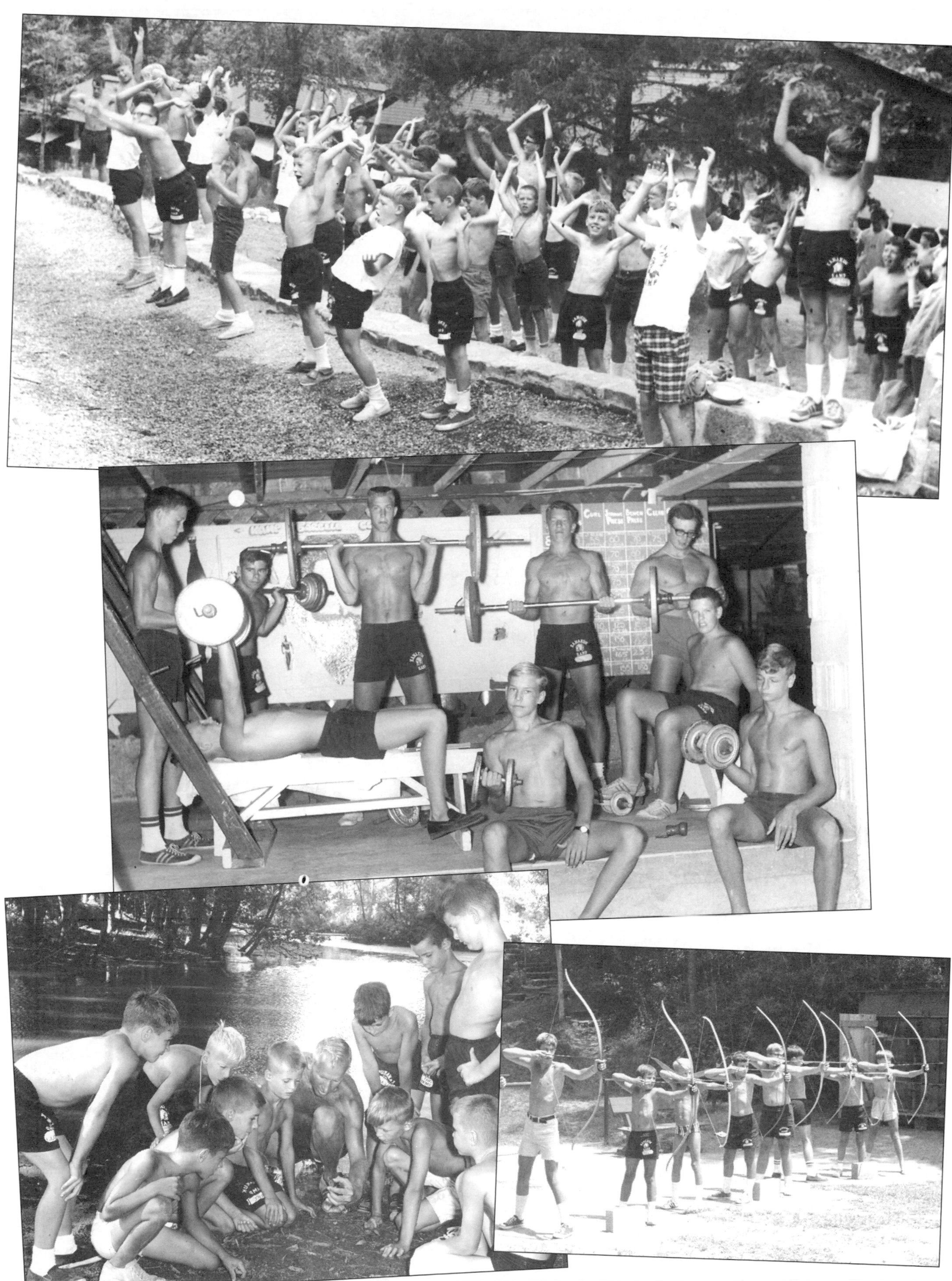

Kamp T-Shirts and Shorts

This shadow-box framed display tells the story of what was "IN" style at summer camps. Orders for camp clothing for both Kamps were mailed to Kamp before Kampers arrived. The Office gals filled the orders in individual brown paper grocery bags in the back of "Old Mess." Sizes and numbers on the orders were the only selections needed. "Keep it simple the Kanakuk way" as Spike was prone to say. Maroon and white were Spike's favorite colors for shorts and shirts (Texas A& M).

After breakfast the second day of Kamp and after Cabin Clean-Up, the Kampers, a cabin at-a-time, lined up at "Old Mess" to receive their Kamp clothing and get their names stenciled on the white block just below the KAMP logo.

In our family, like many other Kamp families with more than one Kamper, when our three sons out-grew the Kamp shorts and "T's," the shorts and shirts were passed on to a brother or sister. The stenciled original name in black ink never really faded too much, but the clothes were worn anyway. As Joe grew bigger, he was wearing Bob's and Bill's labeled "hand-me-downs." Joe was often guilty of leaving and losing his stuff scattered around Kamp: at the pool, down on the lake front, on Kamp trips in back of the truck. . . you name it! Points were taken off the Tribal Charts whenever a Kamper was sent to retrieve socks, shoes, or individual gear. Bob and Bill many times, were singled out to pick up Joe's stuff because their names were labeled on the scattered items.

Years, and even a generation later, erstwhile Staff members have come back to visit wearing their tired and worn Kamp shorts as they look around and reminisce. Several counselors on staff have pleaded to be sold their old worn shorts. Collectors' items! A few deals, I know for sure, were transacted between the two generations!

Moral:
Don't toss out Kamp "oldies"
be it shorts or memories, once treasured. Priceless!

Above:
Kampers attend church.

Right: Devoted Staff.

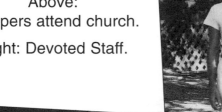

Left: Spike and Darnell's grandsons, Cody, Lance, Scott and Wesley.

Dr. Dick Baldwin
Remembers his friend, John Benien

Dr. Dick Baldwin was a model Kamper, winning Honor Kamper and other awards, and was later a Cherokee Chief during his years at Kanakuk. He returned years later as Kamp doctor. He organized and assembled a playbook for nurses which was used in all the Kamps. Dick Baldwin remains a loyal and serving doctor at the Kamps.

He has been Kamp doctor at K-Colorado, and also travels to Branson to serve in other Kamps the same years. I asked Dick to write about his friend and co-Kamper, John Benien.)

"John and I started Kamp together in 1952. Our fathers knew each other and that is how I found out about Kanakuk Kamp.

John was physically about 18 months ahead of his peers. He held the Midget Track Record for years because he was so fast and so strong for his age. We all admired him for both his personality and his skills.

I once played in a junior high baseball game with John . He was the pitcher. He struck out so many players that the rest of us almost stopped wearing our gloves when we took to the field.

1954 Honor Cabin

John went to a Catholic high school, but we stayed in touch. We both attended University of Oklahoma, where John played Varsity football , following in the footsteps of his older brother, Paul, who lettered in football. Paul was a Kanakuker, too, and had been a Cherokee Chief.

John was in my wedding while I was still in college, but we lost touch while I was in medical school, and he was in law school. During my internship, we learned of his death while serving in Vietam. His funeral was a wonderful testimony to who John was in Life. Both of his brothers spoke. A houseful of tearful ex-college football players and erstwhile Kanakukers attended. I never think of Kanakuk without thinking of John Benien."

- Dick Baldwin, 2006

(Kanakuk Kamp's new dining hall is named for JOHN BENIEN)

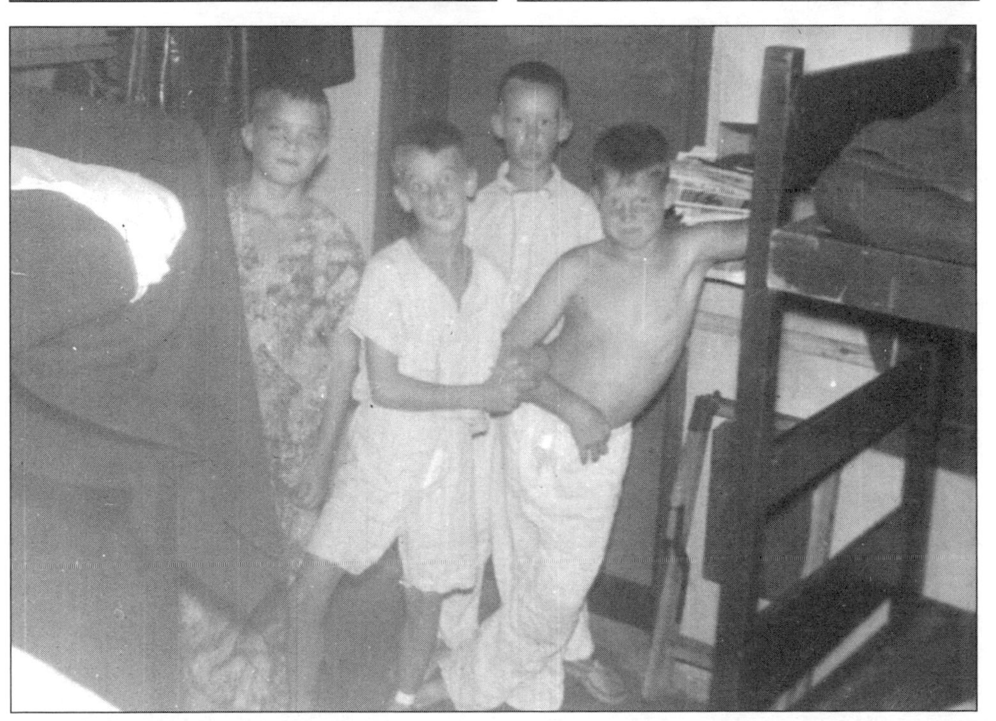

No Swimming Pool

There was no swimming pool (not the kind we see today) at Kanakuk in the early years. There was a "crib" constructed at the lake front where a lot of splashing, free swim and fun was enjoyed. SAMMY LANE RESORT, a nearby resort, had an excellent pool, and through the friendship and hospitality of the owner, Bud Brown (his sons Steve and Mike were Kanakukers), Kanakuk was permitted to conduct swimming, diving, and the First and Final Swim Meets there (with parents attending, also). The Kampers and counselors were shuttled back and forth to SAMMY LANE RESORT in the back of "Big Blue," the Kamp Truck with the big guard rails (scary to think about now!).

Kampers from Kuggaho Boys Camp 1932, posing on the shore of Lake Taneycomo.

One of Spike's top goals included the building of Kanakuk's own swimming pool. In 1957, the pool was constructed. Acquiring Kanakuk's own pool added a finer diminsion and quality to the Kamp. The pool was regulation width and length, and had low and high diving boards, lanes, towers, and a slide. Swim periods were enhanced and safer clinically on Kamp premises. Several years later, after both Kamps' growing enrollment and expansion, a second large pool bordering the original pool was built.

Nocus McIntosh, who year-round lived in the log cabin where the hospital at Kanakomo is today, taught at Branson High School across the lake for nine months and joined the Kanakuk staff each summer. Nocus was unique in many ways and a Kamper favorite. He was notches above others, in the eyes of the older Kampers, especially. Nocus and Frank English, gave exciting and hilarious acts with "script" and costumes. These amazing, incorrigible young men thrilled the spectators by performing on the high dive with props. It was breathtaking and awesome entertainment.

(Continued on Page 67)

KANAKUK KAMP

Senior B

200 Yd. Free Style

1st

1957

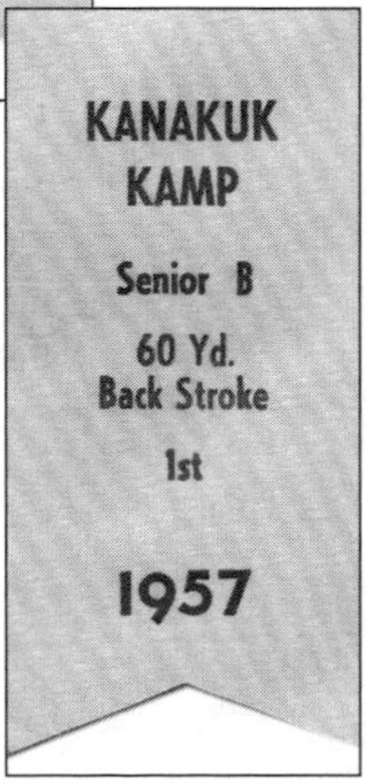

KANAKUK KAMP

Senior B

60 Yd. Back Stroke

1st

1957

(Continued from Page 65)

Words on paper cannot describe the laughter and happy days that made Kanakuk so special. Spike planned a reunion for Coach Lantz twenty years later. Nocus and his cohorts, Frank and Pete English (as agile and talented as in their younger days), returned to perform again, and were every bit as daring and remarkable as in "Days of Yore."

Another event scheduled at the reunion was a track meet: Cherokees vs. Choctaws. The competition was just as heated and the competitors just as determined as they once had been. However, there were no records broken; just a lot of agony and aches, limping and laughter. Men are grown-up boys at heart.

Kanakuk Kamp was (and still is) made up of such wonderful memories and stories.

Nurses at Kanakuk Hospitals

Nurses who give up several weeks in the summertime to administer to the hurts, cuts, bruises, "tummy" aches, homesickness, accidents, Chicken Pox, Measles, sprained ankles and other unexpected inconveniences are angels from above! Through the years the Kamp Hospital has been "Home Sweet Home". The young and the old go there for sympathy, therapy, peace, and tender loving care. It is also a shelter for those with hurt feelings and maybe for the shedding of a few tears, or just a hug. God made nurses very special. Kanakuk Kamps have had a plethora of precious nurses who wear many notches of stewardship and longevity at Kanakuk.

Mary Ritchey and Margaret Pratt for many years drove to Kanakuk and Kanakomo with their Kampers. It was a happy day at the beginning of the Work Week when we saw their station wagon with a Texas license, pulling a big U-Haul trailer and driving through the gate. Like the Tooneyville Trolley, all four doors opened and out poured eight kids and two moms, -- Kanakuk's RNs. All was well when we were assured those delightful and accomplished gals would be at Kamp the whole term! Their doctor husbands were back in Texas rattling around in empty houses and wishing they could be at Kamp, also. Dr. Ritchey often took leave and came to Kanakuk just in time to go on a float trip to get his "Kamp Kicks." When Mary Ritchey died years later, the original Kanakuk Kamp was named for that grand and exceptional lady!

Pat Morrell was another servant nurse for many, many years! She was at least in her late sixties when she stepped down from a long and loving career dedicated and devoted to Kanakuk Kampers. There are many nurses who took off duty on their home fronts to look after the Kampers. Today, many nurses who were once Kanakuk Kampers themselves bring their children to Kamp while they serve in one of the Kamp Hospitals.

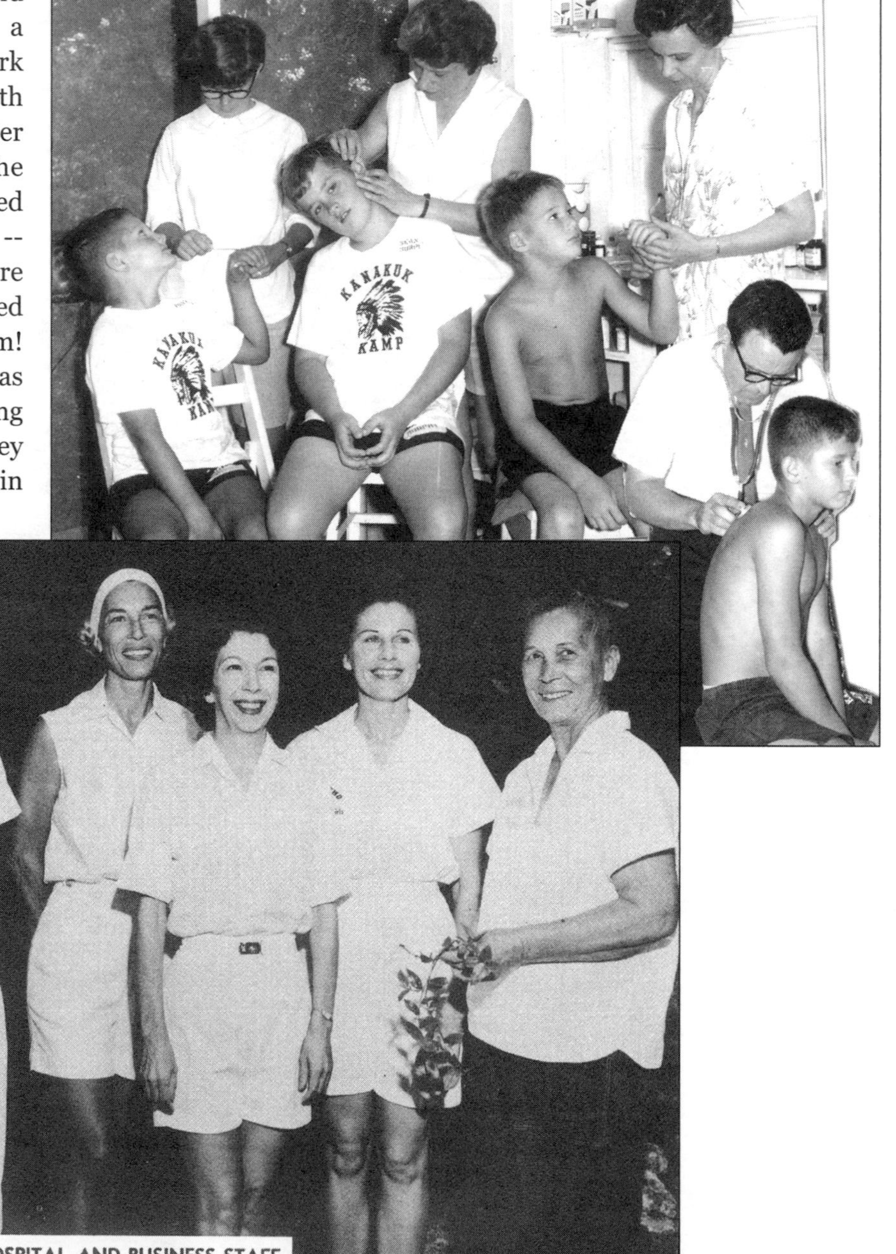

HOSPITAL AND BUSINESS STAFF

"NURSE PAT"

This poem could easily describe each Nurse – as it has for Pat.

Twenty-five years ago Nurse Pat came to Kanakuk and settled in –
Deeper loyalty and love for kids there truly has rarely been –
Nurse Pat is an unsung hero who ministers to Kuk Kampers' ills –
Steady and staunch, tried and true, she is more than just pills –
Cuts, bruises, accidents, rashes, stitches, scrapes, and scabs –
Homesickness, vomiting, fevers, crutches, casts, and sprains -
Trips to the doctor, prescriptions, healing, and easing the pains –
Burning a light while the rest of the Kamp is sound and sleeping –
Nurse Pat is ever medicating, ice-packing, comforting, and keeping –
"Always there" at sick-calls, in-between times, day or late at night –
An angel of Mercy, a surrogate Mom, and a sweet friend of Light –
She's an exhorter, an early-morning starter, a tray-carrier of food –
She's a hugger, a lover, a friend, a servant always in a good mood -
She is a mentor and solace to young Nurses, every "new comer" –
Pat's a prayer warrior, a model of faith, an inspiration all summer –
Kounselors have a special place in their hearts for her "caring" –
Everyone on Staff has a yen for the "Nurse-Pat Fix" and sharing –
Many moons and seasons have scored umpteen countless adulations –
There will be "Stars in her Crown" for her endless Love for Patients.

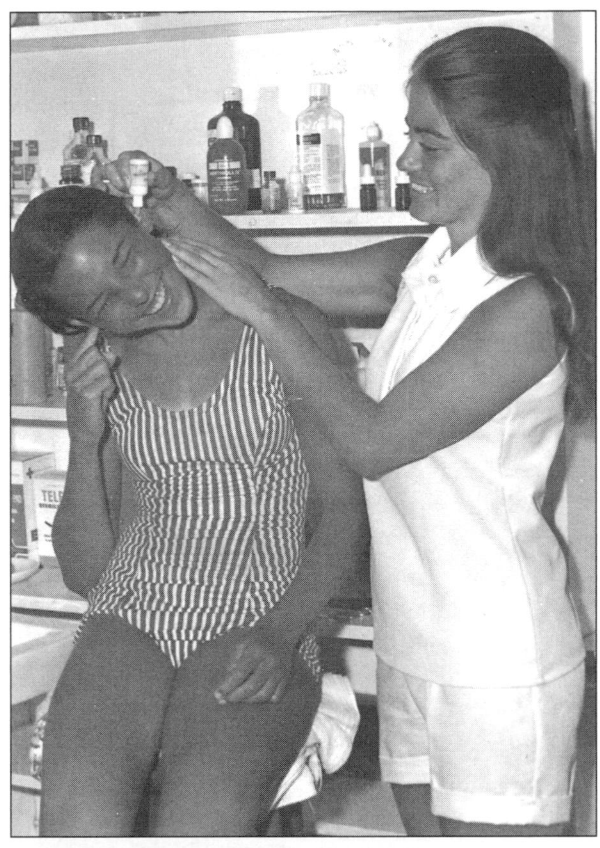

Letter from Scott White, Kamper

G'maw, I cannot wait to read your book! The old Kanakuk is my favorite. Hope this memory helps - it comes from the heart. I do not think that my writing does the memory any justice. But I do want to know that as I think of a single instance that encompasses the whole experience. But since I only get a single page and it is not my book, I will try to keep it short.

I started as a Kamper at Kanakuk at the impressionable age of 6. I was a bit younger than all the other Kampers, but this was permitted because I could walk up the hill and stay at Grandmaw and Pappy's house at night. So each morning I would run down to Kamp and spend the day palling with the older boys of cabin 1. After a big day of fun, I would quietly sneak back to "G'maw's house." This sneaking comes into play later.

One of the great traditions of Kamp is scaring gullible youngsters with stories of the various fiends and monsters that inhabit that particular part of the Ozarks. Within a single square mile you can find the Slough Lady, a notoriously crazy woman what sleeps in the slough and runs rampant at night; the burn victim that can be found lurking in the bathrooms, the Branson Whistler and a few others that come and go through the summers. The fiend that got my goat was the Woolie Monster. I won't go into his various evil deeds or strange habits, but just know that it played on the fears of dumb 6 year old kid.

Even as a youngster I was never very gullible. I had already been through the gullible boot camp with an older brother and a Dad that loved to scare me. I was a skeptic before I could crawl. So, when I showed up at Kamp and heard these tales of lurking villains, it just made me giggle. But something about hearing about them for several weeks and having the stories confirmed over and over by wise counselors gave me enough doubt that my mind started to wonder, "What if just one of the stories were true?"

The Woolie Monster is one of the lesser villains of Kanakuk Kamp. He does not have the fame of the Slough Lady nor the cunning of the Branson Whistler. The reason he became my nemesis that summer is because he lurked the stretch of woods between Kamp and G'Maw's House. So every night I would leave the bright and cheery sounds of Kamp and sneak down the long and dark gravel road to Grandmaw and Pappy's house. As I made my way every shadow looked like a giant hairy beast, every musky smell came from his dirty hide and every sound became his panting.

My greatest memory of Kamp is not some beast that I conjured up or an eternal fear that nags me to this day. My greatest memory is the light in G'Maw's house. It was not a big spot light or a bright siren light. It was a simple light that shone through the little window next to the fireplace; it shone like a beacon against a dark backdrop. And as I snuck down that dark road envisioning that worst kind of torture, I knew that when I saw the light in the window, I was safe. Nothing could hurt me once I reached the light, not even the Woolie Monster.

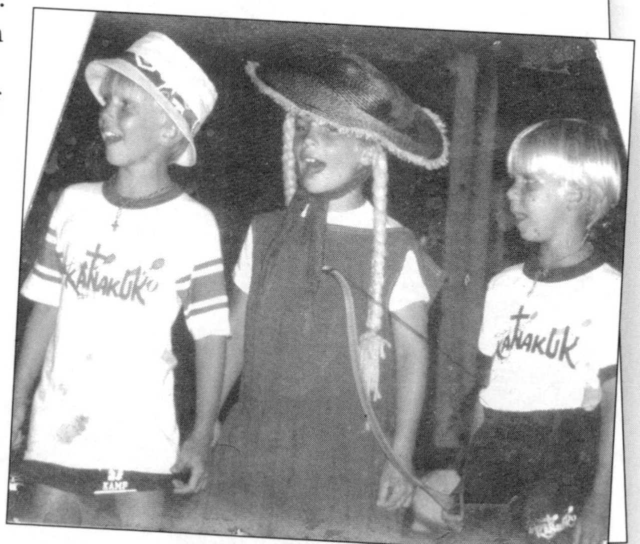

Through the years I had more great memories of Kanakuk Kamp than anyone could ever imagine. At Kamp I was molded into a servant; I was shown what Christ-like character really was. I was taught all of God's great lessons; I was served up humility, gratitude, perseverance and honesty in a four-square meal. But the light on the darkest night is the memory that I will remember the most.

To this very day my favorite part of going back to Kanakuk is the drive up that gravel road and seeing the light in that little window of G'Maw's house.

Because behind that light are my heroes. The kind of people that make you feel safe and welcome.

The Evil Spirit Torments the Good Indian
(This Story happened at The Final Ceremony at Kanakomo Kamp)

Written by Lance White

The Final Ceremony at each of the Kanakuk Kamps is a much anticipated event. It is an exciting time when families, counselors, leadership and Kampers learn which Tribe's Flag will fly higher in the next Term, the following year. This tradition continues today; however, since the Flagship Kamp and original ceremony began with the first Boys' Kamp and the first Girls' Kamp, the Ceremony remains loyal to its roots and foundation. As a result, if a mistake or mishap at this solemn and staunch event occurred, it would not be taken lightly! This story is from the mind and eyes of the person (ME!) who was the brunt of a joke.

It was the end of the 26-day, second Term session at Kamp Kanakomo. The crowd awaited the beat of the "tom-tom" and the Chief Indian who would approach through a gauntlet of silent spectators, then walk up the steps to the top of the rock platform. There, three flagpoles – each Tribal Flag and the American Flag – fly everyday during Kamp; the Winning Flag flies higher than the losing Tribe's flag and not as high as the American flag. When the fountains magically ceased, the Chief Indian would then give the traditional speech that all past Chief Indians had delivered for over fifty "snows-to-snows." Things were going along smoothly at that point on that momentous day and time. I began to beat the "tom-tom" for the Kiowa Princess and the Kickapoo Princess to slowly approach their ascent up the steps to join me at the flagpoles. *THEN* something went terribly awry!

The three leather strands that held up my breech cloth broke simultaneously, and down fell my breech cloth to my ankles! There I stood flabbergasted in my nakedness. The engrossed and watching crowd slowly began to recover from the shock, and through their laughter, the camera flashes, and video cameras rolling, the reality hit hard and my wits slowly took over. I knew that the show must go on. It would not be appropriate to run away from such an important event. My role demanded model behavior.

So, I did what any good Indian would do; I picked up my breech cloth and tried to make it stay by tucking it into the band of my speedo. The Indian apron fell immediately to the ground. Plan B took over: I put the drum in front of my speedo and kept beating the "tom-tom" as the Princesses approached the Fountain. Quickly, I stopped Plan B to go to Plan C: squat down real low and continuing to beat the drum until I settled on the ground. This worked briefly; however, I did not exactly look like a respectful and commanding Chief (more like a whipped Indian hovering over the drum on his lap.)

After what seemed an eternity, a friend, David (Kanakomo's Big Brother) came up with for a solution to the problem. He threw me a towel that he had grabbed from on the Girls' Cabin clothesline. With gratitude, I wrapped the towel around me. This was a HUGE relief.

After I somehow regained my dignity, I continued to beat the drum until the Princesses walked to their appointed spots in front of the Tribal Flags. Then, as a follow-up to the prior "entertainment," I gave the next part of the Indian speech but tweaked it as I spoke about the evil spirits' nature to torment the Indians on any opportunity. I do not know what Tribe won that Term. Now, as I document what happened years ago, it is definitely a blur. It is a buried picture and a memory away.

Then, as a follow-up to the prior "entertainment," I gave the next part of the Indian Speech but tweaked it quite a bit as I spoke about the evil spirits' nature to torment the Indians on any opportunity.

The Rest of the Story: Though I had believed those leather laces had somehow all snapped loose, it was completely false. A year later the real truth, through Kris Cooper, my hero, friend and personal prankster, was disclosed. The Trip men of K-1 had been in on it. The laces had been clipped and their plan was to reach out and yank the cloth as I walked through the crowd to the Fountain. It turned out much spicier. As I was standing high on the Fountain after the cloth fell and was struggling for a miracle, I realized the spectators laughing the hardest were the Trip Men! They were convulsed in laughter, and a spark of suspension kindled my mind. The lesson learned: the evil spirit that I talked about in my altered speech was actually about the mischievous spirit found with the Kanakuk Counselors, those who had been around enough to be so bold as to throw kinks into the most sacred and meaningful Final Ceremony.

Stranger Things Have Happened...

One summer a couple of weeks before Kamp's Opening Day, the Staff of counselors, Directors, kitchen help, and maintenance were busy "spiffing up" the grounds, planting flowers, scouring the kitchen and dining area. storing groceries, catorizing sports equipment, filling the swimming pool, and on and on, when a fine-looking gentleman, accompanied with two boys, ages 10 and 12, approximately arrived. The office girls were making charts, and I looked up to see who had entered. I introduced myself, thinking they were probably early Kampers looking around or tourists looking us over. The man introduced his boys gave his name and with a few "ahems" and "uhs," (it was obvious something was amiss) and asked, "When does Kamp open?" The man had flown to Branson from Colorado to bring his sons to Kamp, which at that time, was two-weeks away! Right away it occurred to me by the look on his face that "someone" had given him the wrong date. I hoped it wasn't his wife! He was embarrassed and mumbled that they would return to Colorado and be back in two weeks! Meanwhile one of Office girls slipped out to find Spike. We convinced the Dad if he would permit the boys to stay with us and be a part of getting Kamp ready, it would be great for all of us. So, the boys hung out early with our boys and the Staff. Probably the most fun-summer those boys ever had!

Conversely, one summer at the end of the Final Week when all parents and grandparents had come and gone, there remained one Kamper from Cabin Two: Skippy (last name not mentioned). Skippy was probably a "home alone-boy" most of the time, and the experience of Kanakuk had done wonders for this super hyper boy. His Counselor was Barney Welch. All summer Barney had us laughing when telling about Skippy's energy and busy behavior: half the time at rest period Skippy would be in the rafters above his bunk... always moving, never still. So, there was Skippy not being picked up, and no word from his mom. I tried to contact his mom and could not locate her.

Barney, Jane, Spike and I laughed and questioned which of us would be taking Skippy to our Texas homes for the winter. A couple of days later, the MOM called and with reluctance said she would be in Branson to take Skippy home. It was a sad day for Barney, Jane, Spike and me thinking that Skippy might be better off if he could have winter in Texas with us.

Kris Cooper, Kuk's Wheaties Champion

Kris Cooper is a Kamper's forever-hero. Kris has a gentle, sweet spirit and a heart big enough to include every boy in Kamp. He knows every boy's name from the first day he walks through the Kanakuk Gate. He has no favorites; in fact, he takes extra time to learn the heart and feelings of each Kamper. It is uncanny the bonding and building of comfort and joy Kris emulates and fills in each boy. Kris is the Director of Kanakuk Kamp, the first Kamp that began in 1926. He is too good to be true! He exudes energy and exciting playfulness and runs an inimitable program of skills in sports, competition, and "just for fun" games. He is a perennial youth!

At breakfast in the dining hall one summer, someone noticed on a Wheaties box that a contest was being held: "Send in one box top of Wheaties, sign the name of a person who is worthy of being a Wheaties Champion, and the most box tops for that person for the summer, ending August 31, would be announced. A picture of the contest winner would be on the Wheaties Cereal Box for a year."

From that day and every day the rest of the summer, Kampers refused to eat any other cereal. Coupons piled, Kampers wrote home to get parents and brothers, sisters, friends to eat Wheaties, save the box tops, and vote for Kris Cooper!" Well, you guessed the rest of the story. However, Kampers were very disappointed and disillusioned although they "knew" who really should be the Wheaties Champion. And KRIS COOPER still IS - in the hearts of all of us.

Back Row: Jim Brawner, Lamar Trishman, Doug Goodwin
Front Row: Brad Dolloff, Kris Cooper and Craig Langamier

THE ORDER OF THE DAY

6:30 – Reveille. – Dip or Shower.

7:00 – Breakfast.

7:30–8:00 – Police Cabins For Inspection.

8:00–10:00 – Instruction in Riflery, Tennis, Nature, or Archery.

10:00–11:00 – Exercises, Track Work, etc.

11:00–12:00 – Swimming, Diving, + Life Saving Instruction.

12:30 – Dinner.

1:00–2:00 – Rest Period.

2:00–4:30 – Tribal Compretion in Base Ball, or Volley ball. (Junior + Senior Groups)

4:30–6:30 – Open for swim, tennis, canoeing, scout work, etc. Wood work instruction.

6:30 – Supper. 7:00–8:00 – Free.

8:00–9:00 – Campfire. 9:00 – Taps.

CHEROKEE
KANAKUK-KANAKOMO KAMPS
19 26
LEVEL LITTLE-K
CHOCTAW
KICKAPOO
KANAKUK-KANAKOMO KAMPS
19 26
LEVEL BIG-K
KIOWA

Kanakuk Kamps and Kin

Our three sons have indelible influences and memories of Kamp because they "grew up" around it and as part of it, physically, emotionally, and spiritually. It runs in their veins. Kanakuk Kamps was our "bread-and-butter," as well as the caring, sharing, and contributing that the business created in the off seasons all blended with the living, playing, and bonding of friendships and relationships formed in the summer months. Kanakuk Kamps was a member of the White Family.

This summer, 2006, when I decided to write stories and history of Kanakuk Kamps, Joe, Debbie Jo, and our other sons and wives have encouraged me. Bob calls daily and asks about the latest I have been writing. Many times he tells me a story that gives me encouragement and "eye and self-witness" information. Bill is our middle son and his "Wild Willie" personality is always refreshing and entertaining. Bill also has suggested stories of Kanakuk summers at Kamp for "patches of the past." Every family should have "one Bill"; more than one would be too many!

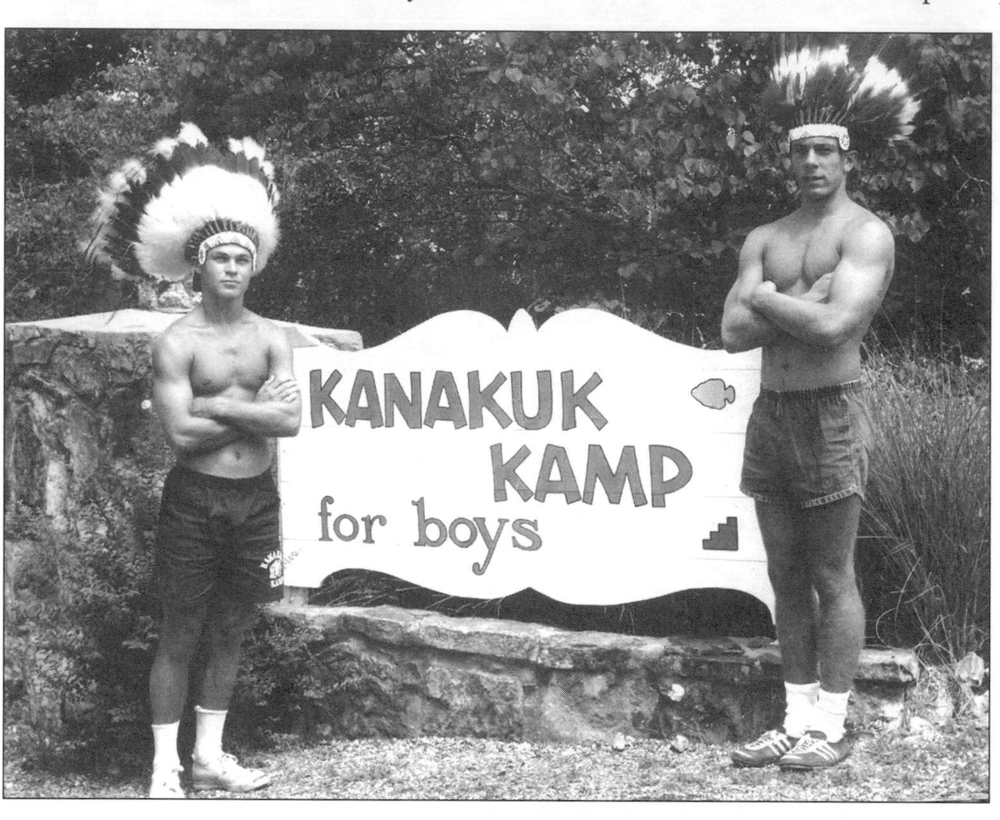

Bill was Chief of the Cherokees, as was Joe, and each was a good Chief-leader, leaving the Cherokee Flag to be flown all summer the following summer until the closing of another year. Bill served as a "Work Boy" the summer before he attended TAMU where he graduated. In those days, Kanakuk had a couple of "work-boys" who performed different jobs of maintenance: collecting and emptying trash, watering, raking, mowing, cleaning the "mutts" and a plethora of other necessary jobs. Bill, near the end of the term, had his night off, and went with another "work-boy" to Rockaway Beach, where he got into a fight with some locals.

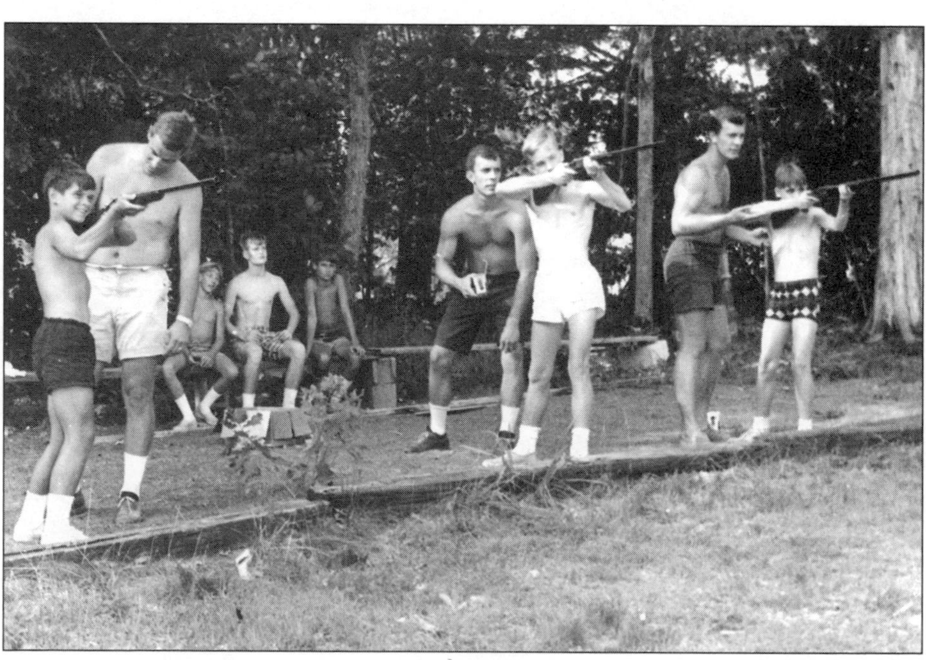

Above:
Dick Patton and Bill White.

Right:
Middle counselor, Bill White,
far right Bob White.

The next morning, Spike came to the office and said, "Darnell, pack what you really need to take, you and Bob (Bob had just returned by air at Springfield, having toured Europe with a College Group under Bob and Bev Braley) need to drive home as soon as possible. Jane will help pack everything after you leave. I'll finish the rest, put Kamp to bed, and drive home."

I had heard about the fight that Bill was involved in. At 4:30 a.m. Spike had gone to the work-boys' cabin in order to get them to help load several canoes. Spike awakened Bill to find Bill's nose bandaged with Popsicle sticks. Mrs. Oglesby, the Kamp nurse, had given Bill first aid after he returned to Kamp. I did not question the decision Spike made. He, as was always his policy, would be meeting the whole Staff as soon as we drove out the Gate. Spike never allowed mystery or rumors spread through Kamp. He addressed everything, "nipping them in the bud."

Spike had made rules, and the fact that this one concerned his own son, was no exception. Spike never "fired" a counselor, he simply "sent the counselor home." Period. Bob recalled, when he was on Staff, seeing another counselor standing at the entrance gate, holding his duffle bag and other gear for a "going-home-counselor." When the meeting was ready to convene, and Spike, in his simple-to-the-point way, informed the Staff of the circumstances, he dismissed them, and that was that! Spike was fair, he was honest, and you could depend on this "Man of his word." The Rule that Bill (and another worker) had broken was understood. "Any person" breaking the rules (including Spike's own sons) would be packing, out the front gate, and "being sent home."

Meanwhile, Bob, Bill and I were on our way to Texas. Each of us was anxious, not knowing what Bill's penalty would be aside from being sent home. Spike always tried to control his emotions and not act in haste and regret, make retributions and judgements until considered with a clear mind-set. That disciplineship had more effect on the family than the end penalty proposed. We had a good, fun trip and stopped in Oklahoma to spend the night. Just before we parked the car, out-of-the blue came reality, and I said, "Hey, Spike fired me, too!" It dawned on me! Spike had kicked me out, too. I guess that realization was partly true. There wasn't a "home to go to" if neither Spike nor I were not there. I have heard our sons say, "We would have been disappointed if Dad didn't discipline us."

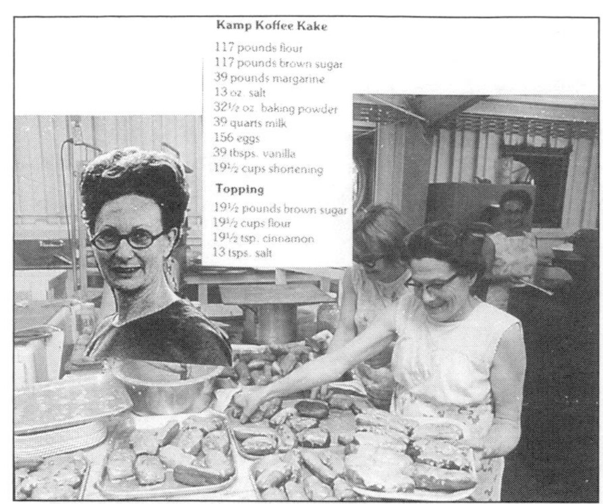

Kamp Koffee Kake
117 pounds flour
117 pounds brown sugar
39 pounds margarine
13 oz. salt
32½ oz. baking powder
39 quarts milk
156 eggs
39 tbsps. vanilla
19½ cups shortening
Topping
19½ pounds brown sugar
19½ cups flour
19½ tsp. cinnamon
13 tsps. salt

Kamp Koffee Kake

Undoubtedly, one of the Top Ten items at Kanakuk Kamps is Kamp's Koffee Kake. Sunday morning breakfast is the very best breakfast to Kampers and Staff. Kampers usually go back home asking Mom to make coffee cake "like they do at Kamp."

Kanakuk Koffee Kake was being baked at Kanakuk before Spike and I purchased the Kamp. One of the two ladies, I think her name was Esther Driskoll from western Oklahoma, brought the recipe to Kanakuk, and now every cook who works here in the summer learns to bake the coffee cake. This recipe has been honed down for a normal-size family. "Try it. . . .you'll like it!"

Recipe for Kanakuk Koffee Kake

(home size)

(Thanks to Gina Hinch – Food Services Manager)

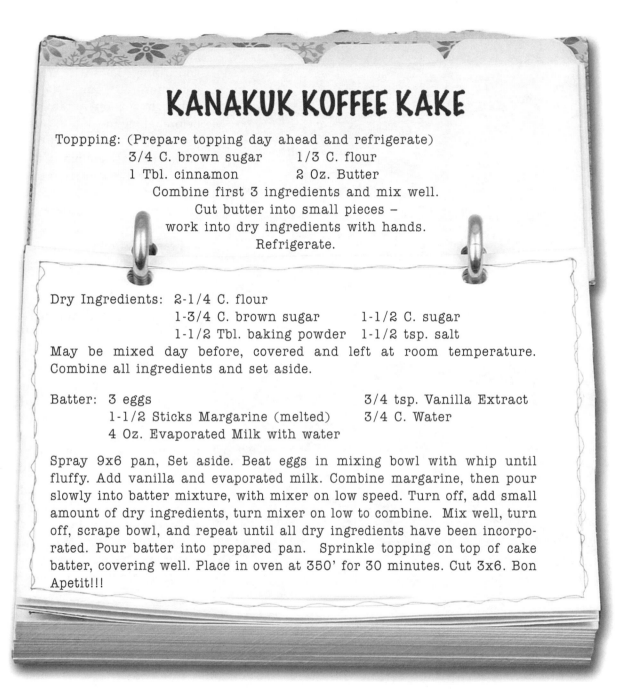

KANAKUK KOFFEE KAKE

Toppping: (Prepare topping day ahead and refrigerate)

3/4 C. brown sugar 1/3 C. flour
1 Tbl. cinnamon 2 Oz. Butter

Combine first 3 ingredients and mix well.
Cut butter into small pieces –
work into dry ingredients with hands.
Refrigerate.

Dry Ingredients: 2-1/4 C. flour
1-3/4 C. brown sugar 1-1/2 C. sugar
1-1/2 Tbl. baking powder 1-1/2 tsp. salt

May be mixed day before, covered and left at room temperature. Combine all ingredients and set aside.

Batter: 3 eggs 3/4 tsp. Vanilla Extract
1-1/2 Sticks Margarine (melted) 3/4 C. Water
4 Oz. Evaporated Milk with water

Spray 9x6 pan, Set aside. Beat eggs in mixing bowl with whip until fluffy. Add vanilla and evaporated milk. Combine margarine, then pour slowly into batter mixture, with mixer on low speed. Turn off, add small amount of dry ingredients, turn mixer on low to combine. Mix well, turn off, scrape bowl, and repeat until all dry ingredients have been incorporated. Pour batter into prepared pan. Sprinkle topping on top of cake batter, covering well. Place in oven at 350' for 30 minutes. Cut 3x6. Bon Apetit!!!

Kanakuk Office Girls "Say Cheese"

Above: Office girls at the home of Sherry Herschend's mother.

Attending American Camp Association Conference, I learned how to hire Office Girls, how to remember names of Staff members, parents and their progeny, how to order camp clothing, amounts and sizes, Award Ribbons and Medals, groceries, take bids, work with the Cooks and Dining Hall Girls. Walsie Ray was a good-natured and fantastic Cook although she often ran out of staples before telling me until it was time to prepare a meal. I urged her to let me know before the last amount was being used. Each time I asked (trying to encourage her to be responsible and independent), "How much shall I order?" With a happy and secure smile, Walsie always answered, "It takes a lot!" I gave up and counted my blessings for her cooking talents and sweet spirit.

Selecting Office Girls was a natural! In our home I conducted a Class in Modeling and Manners to High School Girls, which gave me as a goods source, as well as having lived at College Station so many years and having friends and acquaintances through School, Church and Community. My very best friend from my own teen-age years in Dallas also lived in College Station. Phil and Sara June Goode's four girls and our three boys were about the same ages. Three of the Goode girls (the youngest was a kamper at KOMO) worked in the Kamp Office.

In the Month of May, Spike drove to Kamp long before School was out for the Summer. My office gals and three sons

drove with me to Kamp in the Kamp Station Wagon. The long 11-hour drive to these Ozarks Hills was a long, laughing, lively drive with many "pit stops" for snacks, sodas, and stretching.

Office Girls were a mainstay in the operation. Their fresh enthusiasm made many chores light labor. They covered the gamut of out-of-the-ordinary jobs to have prepared for the Opening of Kamp and made it a "big deal." Charts for Chiefs, Charts for Cabin Clean-up, Charts for Competition, Charts for Knot-tying, Charts for Passing Trees, Charts for Toothbrush Check-ups mostly were done outside the Office where the Girls acquired a good start on suntans.

During Work Week Spike gave driving lessons to the Office Girls: how to drive Pick Ups while using the gear-shift (no automatic cars)

Our highly skilled and efficient OFFICE GALS having a picnic—as usual

in these Ozark Hills, as well as the importance of staying within range behind Spike when transporting Float Trippers in these Ozark Hills. An office girl would drive a pick-up truck loaded with camping gear and food and often pulling a trailer of canoes. The Office Girls were eager, enthusiastic, excited, and ready for any errand or special trip. Float Trippers rode in the back of "Old Blue."

Driving to the "put in" places wasn't on four-lane Highways. The "shunpike" and narrow, rough, hilly, rocky roads demanded a driver's concentration, and, as if that wasn't enough, keeping up with Spike was an all-time challenge. Kanakuk Kamps, in later years, owned buses for these excursions. (Erstwhile Kampers to this day brag about their adventures riding in the back of "Old Blue.")

Every summer when the Kamp photographer took pictures, the Office Gals, Jane Welch, (my years-long friend and wife of Barney), and I found unique places and props for our picture, hoping to be selected for the catalog. Once Cheri Bonsteel climbed a tree to sit on the tree limb that hung over the battered old flat boat we found down in the slough. Jane, the other girls, and I were in the boat below Cherie. At the precise moment the picture was snapped, the limb broke and down fell Cheri into the boat, and we all swamped! We have pictures caught in the act!

Kanakomo Born and Name Chosen

At our home in College Station there was a round table in the kitchen that was the center of many meetings, doing homework, and sitting down for coffee with a neighbor or my special friend, Sara June Goode. We are still "pen pals" and have shared most of our lives since 1936. She is a lively and clever correspondent at the age of 94. Her daughters have been a part of both Kanakuk (working in the Office) and Kanakomo.

Spike had a penchant for all members of the family having one meal (at least) together. The evening meal was timed to coordinate with school athletics, Spike's work, or any unusual interruptions. It was not unusual for games to be played or riddles while we ate. It sounds cozy and ideal; however, the rules were broken sometimes. We were normal to the hilt! We tried! In fact, I probably was akin to many Kamp Moms: I looked forward to summers when our own three sons would be Kampers and under the influence and guidance of Kanakuk Staff who administered to Youth, thinking Kanakuk could do more than I was able to give.

During an evening meal in the Fall of 1957, Spike threw out a challenge to us: "What do you think would be a good name for the Girls' camp?" Names were spurted out around the table, some ludicrous, some silly. Spike sternly let the boys know that this was serious business. Everyone got the message and seriously tried "thinking of a name." Bill yelled out *"Kanakomo!" Kana because of Kanakuk, and Komo after Lake Taneycomo. Sounded great to each of us. Spike said, "Let's go for it!"

*Branson is in Taney County - CO for County MO the abbreviation of the State of Missouri.

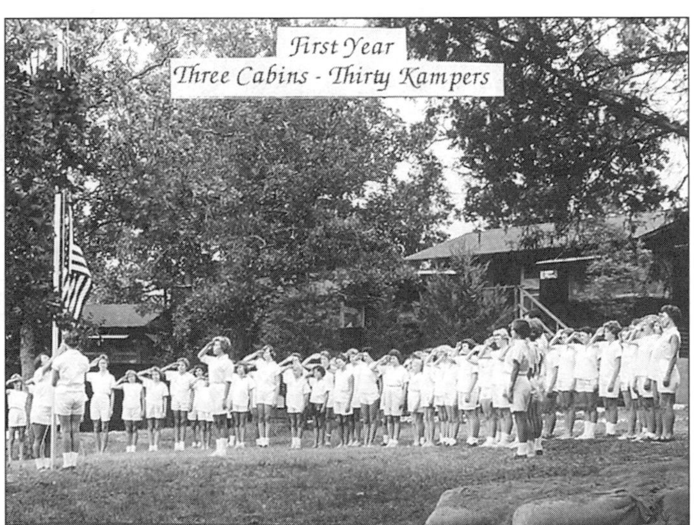

"Girls at Kanakuk?"
"No, A Sister Kamp, Kanakomo"

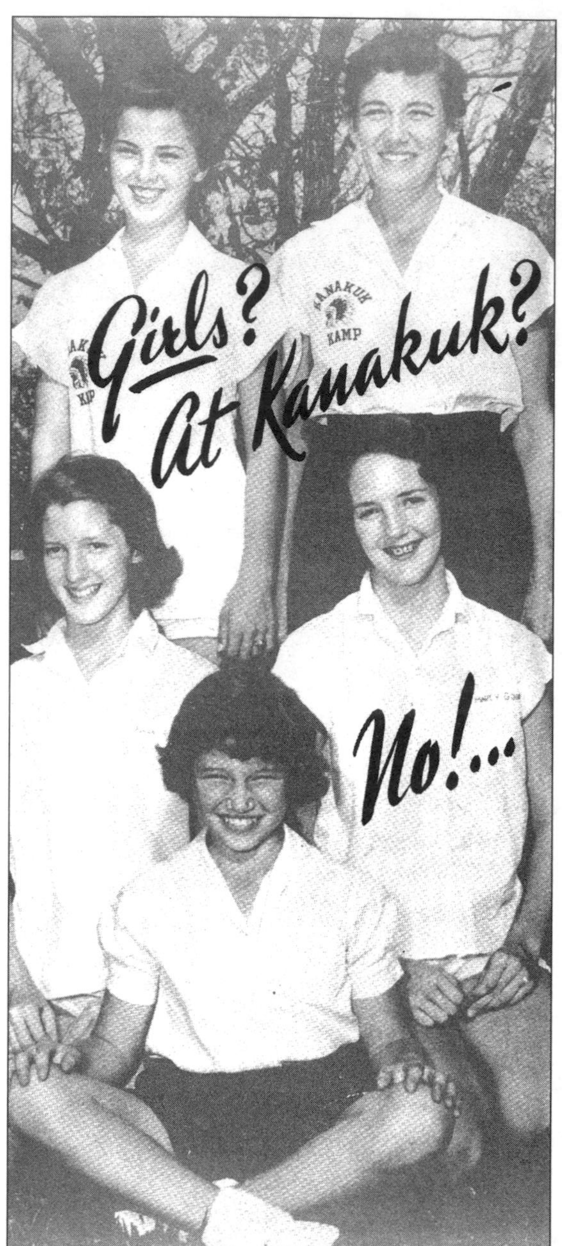

It was the last and final Canoe Meet in 1956, and Coach Lantz and Spike were watching on the sidelines. As the meet was being cheered on by the parents and too-young-for-Kamp siblings, Coach Lantz noticed something. There were many girls in the audience who were Kamp age. "Uncle Bill" leaned close to Spike and asked, "Look around, what do you see?"

Spike was at the drawing board that next fall and winter, and the plan for a Girls' Kamp was in the making! Our friends, Sara June and

Phil Goode, had four girls, and Spike used them in the advertising campaign announcing Kamp Kanakomo for Girls in 1958.

Cabins for thirty girls were ready the first year. Many of the girls were sisters of brothers who were Kanakukers or second generation daughters whose Dads were Kanakukers.

Manley Vance, a school teacher in Liberty, Missouri had been a counselor at Kanakuk a couple of years, and his maturity and worthiness was outstanding. His wife, Lenna, and their three daughters came with him each summer, living in a house in Branson, while Manley was on

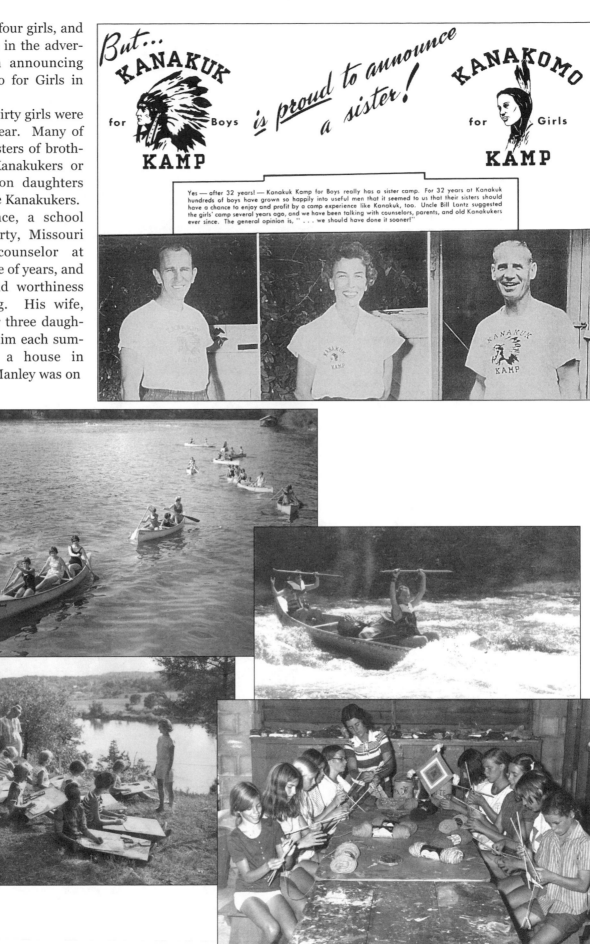

But...
KANAKUK
for Boys
KAMP
is proud to announce a sister!
KANAKOMO
for Girls
KAMP
Yes — after 32 years! — Kanakuk Kamp for Boys really has a sister camp. For 32 years at Kanakuk hundreds of boys have grown so happily into useful men that it seemed to us that their sisters should have a chance to enjoy and profit by a camp experience like Kanakuk, too. Uncle Bill Lantz suggested the girls' camp several years ago, and we have been talking with counselors, parents, and old Kanakukers ever since. The general opinion is, " . . . we should have done it sooner!"

staff at Kanakuk. Manley had all the fine qualities and character to be a leader with boys and girls. It was a natural choice to select Manley Vance to direct the Girls Kamp. Their first daughter, Vicki, was old enough to be a Kamper the first year, and the other girls would soon follow. Lenna was a school teacher, also, and her qualifications, mostly her gentle and caring spirit, made her the ideal partner for Manley's staff and Kanakomo's benefit.

On the Winter Movie Trail, Spike advertised Kamp Kanakomo, and many girls signed up for the Grand Opening. The first Princess of the Kiowa Tribe and the Princess for the Kickapoo Tribe

were selected as Spike observed the personalities and talents of the teenage girls as he talked with their parents on the trail.

Nell Rogers and Jane Berry were selected to be Kanakomo's first Princesses, and they were ideal role models for the important and special role. 1958 was an exciting year. The wellspring was flowing.

KANAKOMO KAMP WAS OFF AND RUNNING!

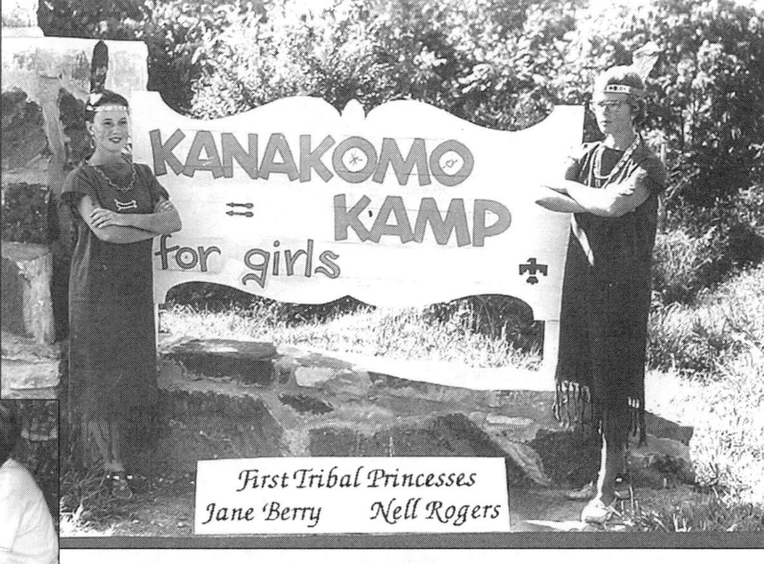

First Tribal Princesses
Jane Berry Nell Rogers

GOLF
As a part of the optional sports instruction program, interested girls are taken to nearby GOLF RANCH where a nationally known golf professional, Don Gardner, provides clubs, balls, and expert instruction.

Ponytail Parthenon

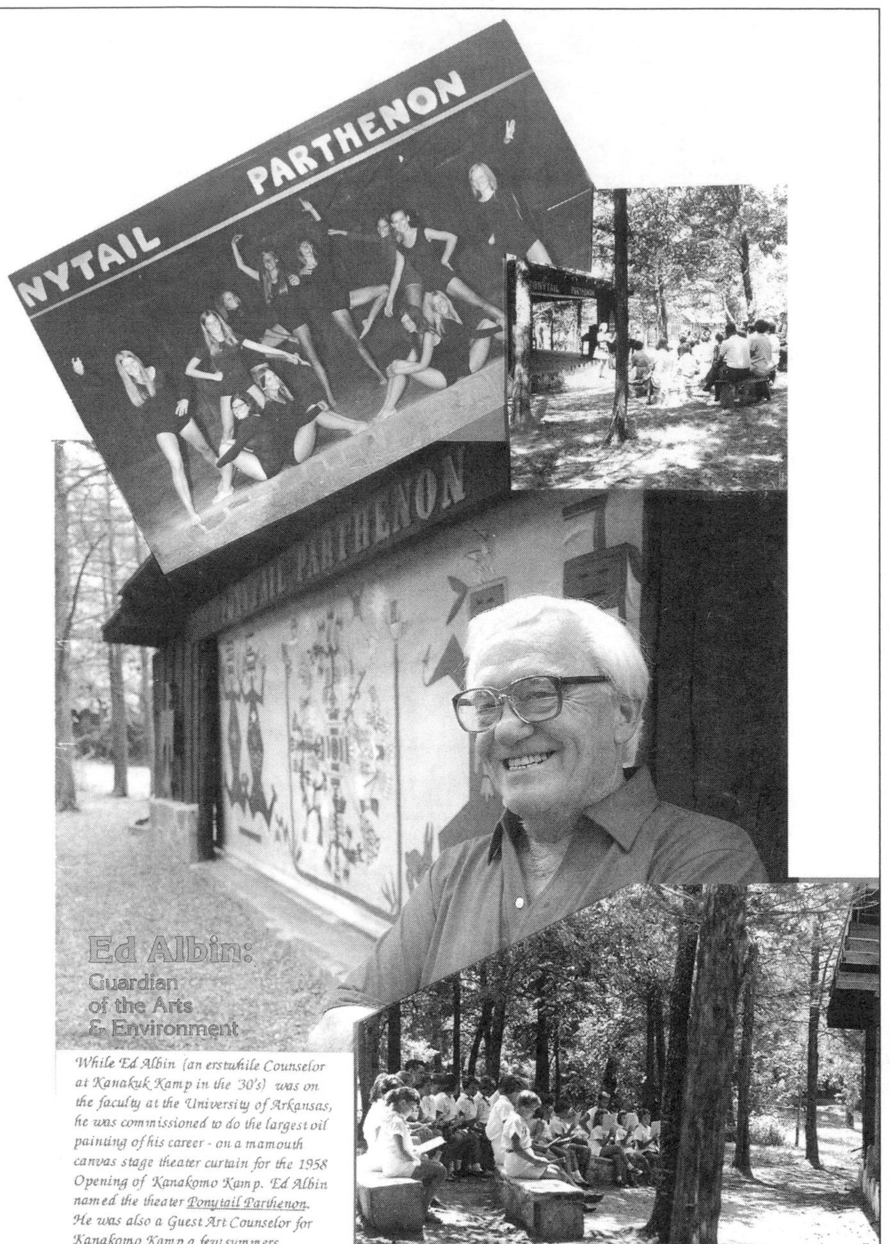

While Ed Albin (an erstwhile Counselor at Kanakuk Kamp in the 30's) was on the faculty at the University of Arkansas, he was commissioned to do the largest oil painting of his career - on a mamouth canvas stage theater curtain for the 1958 Opening of Kanakomo Kamp. Ed Albin named the theater Ponytail Parthenon. He was also a Guest Art Counselor for Kanakomo Kamp a few summers.

Ed Albin had been a counselor at Kanakuk Kamp in late 1930's and '40's. He was on the faculty at University of Arkansas, and was later Head of Deptment of Art at Southwest Missouri State in Springfield, Missouri. He was a delightful and talented, man with creativity and charm. He made the handsome curtain for Ponytail Parthenon where the stage was well used for performances of skits, dance, talent shows, and daily gatherings. Ed Albin also was a Resident Staff Member, giving art classes to the girls. His ingenuity was popular and a boost to the programs offered at Kanakomo Kamp. Sand-drawing and creations were amazing, as were other artwork Ed Albin introduced. The picture shown in this book was made many years after Ed Albin had retired from SMSU. He had returned to Kanakomo to visit his "once-upon-a-times" at Kanakuk and Kanakomo.

"POISE and CHARM"
Darnell White

KANAKOMO

On the shore of Taneycomo
'Mid the Ozark's rolling hills,
Stands a spot apart from others
To which my memory thrills.

'Tis there, both Kickapoo and Kiowa,
When the Spring Moon fills the sky,
Unearth the sacred tomahawk
And shout the battle cry.

Voices ring across the valley
As these friendly warriors fight
To advance their tribal standing
And display their prowess might.

Busy days go swiftly onward
The summer moon begins to wane,
The weapon then is buried —
Until the Spring moon comes again.

Quiet now, the lonely valley,
Only bird calls silence break,
For the warriors have departed
Other battles to partake.

Yet they dream of Kanakomo
And of Kamp, their summer home,
And in memory they linger
On this spot they loved to roam.

Of Lenna, Manley, and Uncle Bob
And "Spike" and Darnell their thoughts fill
And the host of friendly counselors
Each dedicated to this hill —

May the good Great Spirit bless us,
Watch us with loving care;
Help us remember, "I Am Third"
And help us grow "Four Square"

We will need strong, healthy bodies,
We will need minds, clean and firm,
And we'll need good friends and buddies
And to God our hearts will turn.

May each one of us remember
As the moons do wane and rise —
Kanakomo on Taneycomo
And Thy spirit in her skies.

By ED ALBIN, Art Counselor
Professor of Art
University of Arkansas

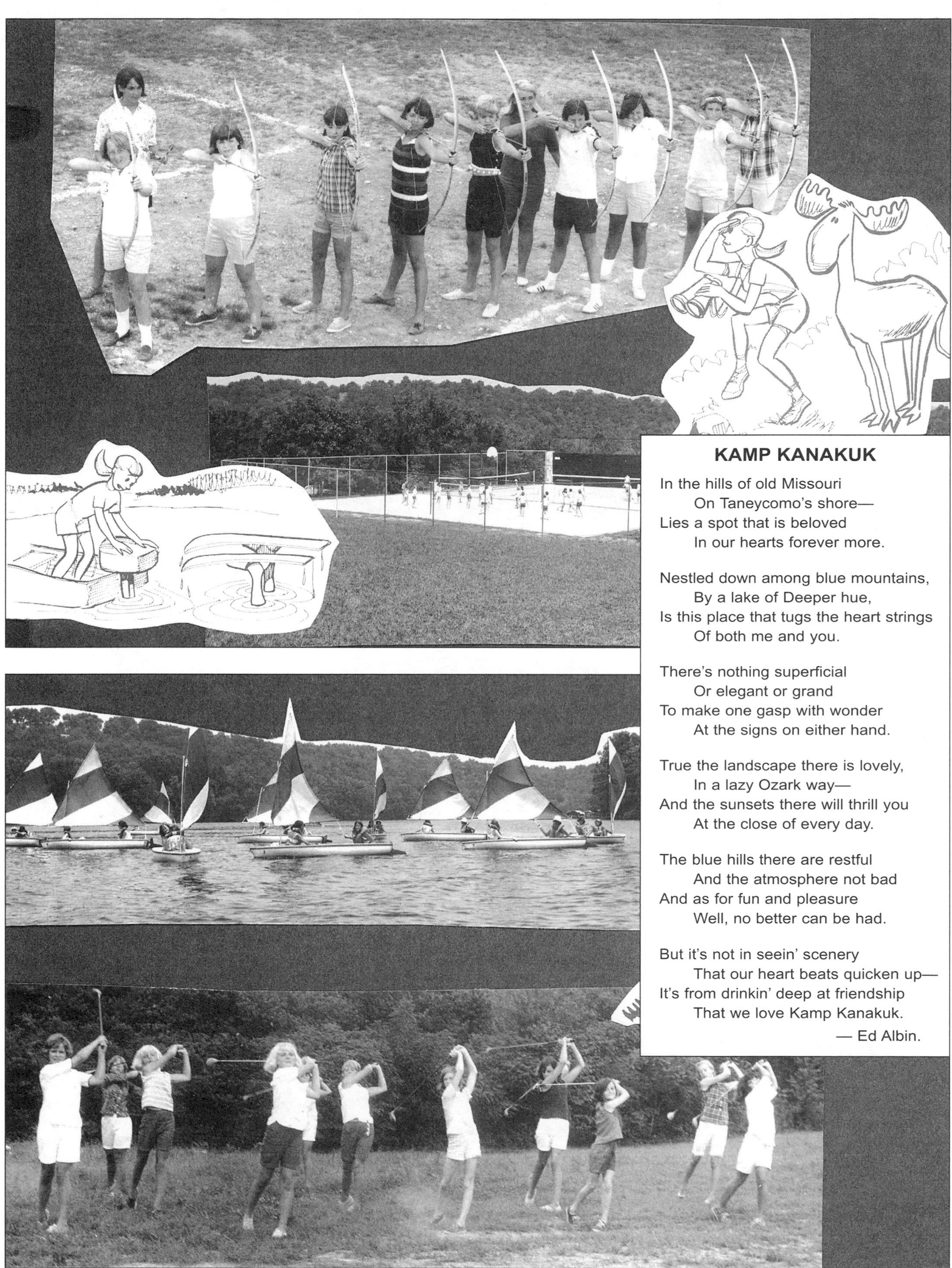

KAMP KANAKUK

In the hills of old Missouri
On Taneycomo's shore—
Lies a spot that is beloved
In our hearts forever more.

Nestled down among blue mountains,
By a lake of Deeper hue,
Is this place that tugs the heart strings
Of both me and you.

There's nothing superficial
Or elegant or grand
To make one gasp with wonder
At the signs on either hand.

True the landscape there is lovely,
In a lazy Ozark way—
And the sunsets there will thrill you
At the close of every day.

The blue hills there are restful
And the atmosphere not bad
And as for fun and pleasure
Well, no better can be had.

But it's not in seein' scenery
That our heart beats quicken up—
It's from drinkin' deep at friendship
That we love Kamp Kanakuk.

— Ed Albin.

Better Wives, Better Mothers: 101

During Work Week at Kanakomo, Spike taught the counselors his course called, "How to be better Wives and better Mothers." Staff didn't "sign up" for the course; it was mandatory, (kinda' like his "You don't have to, you get it to").

One of the favorite subjects, by far, went like this: The young. naive coeds would line up outside of the shower and bath cabin, walk in, and sit astride on the closed lids of the commodes, facing the tanks, then lift off the tank cover. He would then instruct the counselors to look carefully at all the parts as he named and described them. He proceeded to teach them the preliminaries of stopping leaks and the continual running of the water in the tank. The plunger was demonstrated, also. The girls would then go through the procedures afterwards, taking apart, and replacing each part. He told the girls, "More than any other "SOS" in camping was the frantic calls and screaming from the girls, arousing panic and causing mayhem, "Help! the toilets are flooding; the tank water won't shut off!"

Often at Kamp the counselors would tell Spike that it had made them instant heroes because of their hidden talents at saving Kampers from catastrophe. And through the years, the girls have written to Spike that in their homes the knowledge of the comode has been used and agree that it makes them "better Wives and better Mothers."

Spike also said, "Women folks never have enough shelves in the cabins–shelves and coat hangers!" (However, teaching young ladies to hammer and saw was not a part of "Kanakomo 101.")

We Were Family

Kanakuk boasts of Mary Jane Rose who attended Kanakomo from the age of 9 through her graduation from Texas Tech University. She had "Kuk" genes: her Dad had been a Kanakuker. Like father like daughter, she "grew up in Kamp." Little did we know that someday she would become an Opera Dilettante, winning nationally a year's training in New York City under the Direction of Pavarotti. At the end of the year, she was awarded the prestigious privilege of singing with Pavarotti in "La Boheme." Mary Jane travels abroad, as well as stateside, performing with Symphony Orchestras and Santa Fe Festival of Entertainment in the summer months.

At Kanakomo, Mary Jane was called "Mousey" but she was the antithesis of "mousey!" She had a glowing, funny, happy, radiating personality, absolutely wonderfully and specially made! Everyone loved and laughed with Mousy. There were the Jane Gerharts, C.J. Stantons, Gail and K-K Guiders, Janey Ritcheys, Kay Coxs, Judy Spearmans, and the list goes on and on. The Kampers make the Kamp! They return to be Kamp Counselors. Their children become Kampers, and the traditions and tributes continue.

Carolyn Monnet was a Kamper, and Diane Monnet joined her sister when she was 10 years old. Each became Princesses. Their brother Michael was a Chief in the boys' Kamp. There are probably few years, if any, that Diane was not involved with Kanakomo Kamp. Today she directs Kanakomo Kamp. She is married to Kris Cooper (they met in these Ozark Hills), and their wonderful family grew up as "Kamp Kids" as their parents did. The Cooper family is the dream of Counselors who are wanting a family.

In reflection, I am reminded that Spike hired Kay Holliday, Hank Harmon, Suzette and Jim Brawner the same year that Debbie Jo was hired. "It was a very good year." Diane Collins was a Kamper and on Staff when she and Hank met and married. Like others, they chose their vocation in Kamp work: Kanakuk and Kanakomo Kamps. Kay Holliday was Director of the girls' Kamp for several years. Today, Kay is our Ambassador of Kanakuk Kamps. She is everywhere, seems like, "at the same time." Her dedication and devotion to Kamp families is shown throughout the year: visiting hospitals, attending special events, weddings, funerals, touching base with Kampers and Kamper families all over the United States. As the apropos saying goes, "She is one h-a-p-p-y Camper." Everyone loves K-K, and her name is always spelled with a "K"!

Talent, beauty, love, and enthusiastic devotion add up to the PZAZZ of a staff personifying inspiring leadership.

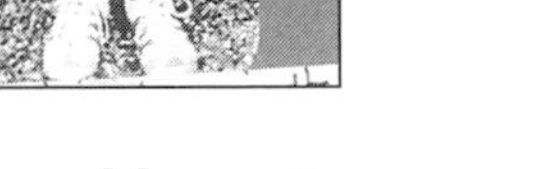

Diane Monnet
Kiowa Princess

"H-A-P-P-Y" KAY

Kay Holliday

Debbie Jo Downs

"It was a very good year!" when Debbie Jo came on Staff at Kanakomo. Debbie Jo was an excellent gymnast and one of the best "teachers" in any sport and whatever she had an avid interest in. Watching her at S.M.U. football games, even before knowing her, Spike and I loved watching her cheer at the games (incidentally, she was the first girl officially designated as Head Cheerleader for Southern Methodist University). Debbie Jo never quit or slacked cheering the team when the Mustangs played. In between routine cheering, she would be standing just a fraction off the line, as close as she could get without being on the field, to watch astutely and intently while sometimes yelling to the team what to do, just like a Coach! They rarely interrupted or "shoo'd" her away. She must have called 'em right! She didn't outgrow it after college days: she rarely misses a good game on television, as she is "coaching and calling the plays."

Debbie Jo was in a Physical Education Class at SMU with several Varsity football players (Joe was one of them). Most of the football players were rarely prepared for class; too tired or too disinterested to answer the professor's questions when called upon. One time Debbie Jo spontaneously blurted out the answers before one of the fellows could respond. The Professor called her down often, "Miss Downs, I know you know the answers, but I want the men to answer." (I don't think she ever stopped; she knew they hadn't studied.)

Debbie Jo and other SMU students were on the list of invitations to attend The Kanakuk Winter Movie Trail at Highland Park Methodist Church just off campus. Spike and I were at the door to greet our Kampers and their friends and families. Joe had asked us to watch for Debbie Jo and to invite her to sit with me during the movies. It was a delightful evening for me to sit with her and get acquainted.

Just off the river trip.

SMU Counselors -Staff 1971
Coach Ray Utley and Team Members

Debbie-Jo and the staff from SMU – Joe White on her right.

Debbie Jo was hired for the summer and has not missed a summer since then. Director Manley Vance would share with us a number of pranks she instigated in Kamp. The picture of Debbie Jo coming off the river from a float trip, holding wild flowers, smiling and looking like a million dollars, is one of my favorite pictures made by Spike. Being brought up in Scottsdale, Arizona, Debbie Jo had not been raised canoeing in rapids or sleeping on a bedroll on Gravel bars. She wasn't use to swamping in a canoe, getting wet by sudden rainfalls or having a tent fall down around her ears. Eating campout food, setting up tents and staying upbeat to encourage Kampers not to gripe was all new!

While they sat watching the gorgeous view below overlooking the Lake... Joe gave her a box of Cracker Jacks, her favorite "snack."

Joe and Debbie Jo were friends all the first summer and kept dating through the next summer at Kamp. Joe got permission from Manley Vance to wake her early one "nearly Dawn" and drive her to the top of Baird Mountain, near Table Rock Lake. While they sat watching the gorgeous view overlooking the lake and seeing Dawn's early light, Joe gave her a box of Cracker Jacks, her favorite "snack." As she "finished off" the Cracker Jacks, she was just in the act of tossing the empty box out and beyond! Joe eagerly grabbed the box just before it was falling over the mountain! He handed the box back to her and reminded her that she hadn't kept the prize at the bottom of the box. It was her engagement ring (nearly a "diamond in the rough"). Joe proposed!

After Debbie Jo graduated the following semester of that second year, they were married in Scottsdale. A couple of nights later, they were joined by Spike on the Winter Movie Trail. "Honeymoon to Hawaii" was put on hold until the Movie Reunions were completed.

After Debbie Jo spent more time in full-time family business, she probably understood better why "Honeymoons" don't get priority timing.

Talent, beauty, love, and enthusiastic devotion add up to the PZAZZ of a staff personifying inspiring leadership.

Gone Fishin'

For three summers during Bob White's SMU and Baylor Dental College career, he worked for Manley Vance at Kanakomo Kamp. One of those summers after Bob and Mary Evelyn married, she also was on Staff. Mary Evelyn ("Mev") taught manners and modeling, as well as assisting in other activities.

> Never say 'it can't be done' to a group of girl Kampers.

Bob taught swimming at the Girls' Kamp. He was a Varsity Swimmer at SMU and qualified. Often I watched Bob coach the girls (he coached them: "Ladies,.................") That was the first time I ever heard our girl Kampers be referred to as "ladies." I thought perhaps Spike and I had done a good job raising Bob. Manley and Bob together chaperoned and supervised the Float Trips and Campouts.

Bob related to me recently about one of the Canoe trips. The floaters had stopped at a gravel bar in the early evening to set up camp for the night. Tents were erected, fires started and the girls scattered about to bring in twigs and small wood findings for the cooks' fire. After eating, Bob was fishing. Kay Cox and Donna Pratt ran up to Bob to show him a trotline Kay had found on the gravel bar. They asked Bob to help them set it out overnight. Bob didn't deflate them one iota when he told them the odds of catching anything on the trotline with its big hook was practically nil. Bob put on a hunk of bologna and appeased their excitement by setting the line out across the other side of the river. The next morning, very, very early, Bob and Manley were awakened by a shouting of laughter and joy. Kay Cox and Donna Pratt were yelling for all the girls to see their Catch! A BIG UGLY CATFISH! (Yes, the Float Trippers had catfish for breakfast!)

Moral: Never say 'it can't be done' to a group of girl Kampers.

Boys Don't Have All The Fun

Bob and Mary Evelyn married in Dallas before Bob attended Baylor Dental College. They came to Kamp two summers as Staff at the Girls' Kamp Kanakomo. "Mev" had oodles of talent and attributes that enhanced the Staff program although she had never been a camper at a Girls' Camp.

The first activity she was assigned to was AERIAL DARTS on the courts down on the lakefront. As she was going down the zigzag trail with another Counselor, Peggy Jane Brazealle, she confided in Peggy Jane, "I have never played Aerial Darts, and I don't know the rules. I hope you do and can teach me."

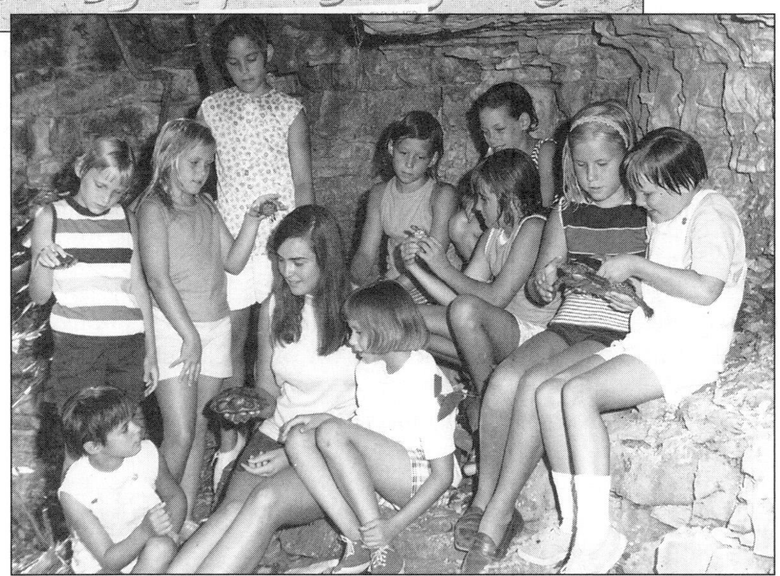

Above: Ann Symington teaching nature class.

Peggy Jane said, "I don't know much more than you do, but let's just wing it, and I will think of something." The Kampers were waiting and Peggy Jane spoke, "How many of you remember playing Aerial Dart from last year?" (Several girls raised their hands.) Peggy Jane nodded with a pleased and proud-of-you-smile and responded, "Mev and I would like for as many as remember the rules to recite them for everyone to review before starting." There were a few girls who were eager to impress their Counselors, and Mev or Peggy Jane soon had an adequate education to begin the two Tribes in a "friendly tribal competition."

Mev, returning to the Cabin after the afternoon activities were over for the day, had a brainstorm. She spoke with Manley about his idea of letting her make a "Tickler File" on each activity with rules, instructions, and other worthy information. From that one observation and knowledge, the "Tickler File" was used with gusto and appreciation from that summer on. Easy to guess who used the Tickler File the most! Mev confided that summer that there were a few other times she encountered brain "blanks" as a Kamp "Rookie." However, she knew Beth Perkins, the professional Kamper who had been a camper for several years, and would "S.O.S" Beth for help. Blessings on Beth!!!! (And a little caper will lead you!)

Mev also taught the classes of "Poise and Charm" that I had been teaching. She was in her element teaching "manners and modeling." Mev added a real "punch" to the program when she contacted the posh Man's Land (a shop in Branson) and attained permission to use their lovely clothing for a Style Show at Ponytail Parthenon at the end of Kamp. Everyone loved it! (The Kampers gave a fine performance despite the tanned legs with bandaids, skinned knees, and "skeeter bites.")

Float trips will always bring out the true grit in any counselor, and Mev scored again because of Judy Booth's discernment. Judy Booth was Head Counselor for many years. Her winsome and clever nature was a boon to the whole Kamp atmosphere and summer experience. The girls, for the first time ever, were "put in" on the Current River, a few hours from Kamp. This river was the favorite and the best adventure in the Program: only older boys were selected for this 10-Day Float trip (that was at the time the term for Kanakuk was 8 and then 7-weeks). The girls were given this privilege when the water on the Buffalo was too low because of not enough rain. Manley and Spike selected the Current River, the only time Girls had been offered this adventure. Mev was scheduled on this trip, with Kanakomo. It was announced that Mev would be in the front bow and Judy in the stern! Mev discerned that Judy was cognizant of Mev's secret woe, and placed her in the bow. At the end of the 4-day float, the trip returning to Kamp was enhanced by the laughing and exaggerated "war stories" of the experiences on the Current. The Girls were given a whole quarter when the Trippers stopped at a Diary Queen. Usually double "dimies" were the epitome of "can't get any better than that."

Float trips probably win "hands down" for the most exciting and interesting stories of long, long ago. It was certainly in reverie of Kampers and counselors and cherished past, present, and future. Bob White and Manley shared a priceless story of one such float trip. After a long day on the James River and after setting up tents for the night, the crew had supper and sat around the fire roasting marshmallows, making smores, and sharing stories. When the girls went to grab a good night's sleep, Manley and Bob settled about 100 yards away and turned in as well. Everything was quiet until a lot of splashing and laughing was heard. Bob came out of his Pup-tent, looked over in the distance where the sounds came from, when Manley joined him. Bob said, "What are they doing? Girls can be so silly; they are out in the river!" Manley marveled at Bob's naivete and said, "Bob, they are "skinny-dipping"and we need to get them out and back to their tents! Locals might be around and we could have some trouble." Bob grabbed some pots and pans and began beating on them while Manley brought out a whistle. Girls were squealing and scampering out of the river and dashing to their tents. It wasn't minutes before that area was quiet and calm. The next morning when called to breakfast, the girls and counselors, looking meek and mild, gathered 'round the fire. There was no talking, but there was an occasional sound of snickering that couldn't be suppressed.

The Counselors often learn more from a Kamp experience than the Kampers!

Stunt Night at Taneycomo Court and Ponytail Parthenon

Like Baskin-Robbins, competition at Kanakuk and Kanakomo Kamps comes in many flavors. The stunts, skits, and stage shows that the Tribes presented at the Kamps were stunning and even brilliant! The skits which created by Kampers and counselors, were hilarious and entertaining, as well as clever, shades of today's Young Life. Cabin stunts were great, and each Kamper acted out the role with earnest zeal. There were One Act Shows, also: talented piano players, dancers, gymnasts, story-tellers, magicians.

STUNT NIGHT was the highlight of the Term for everyone. Before the Girls' Kamp was begun, Kanakuk Kamp had been enjoying and marveling at the stunts and skits the Kampers performed. Winner of the BEST VOTED STUNT presentations by each Tribe received a big number of points toward the Final Count for the Tribe.

At the close of the Term, the Princesses and the Chiefs for the next term, the next year, would be announced at the Final Ceremonies. The Kampers would vote for their selection. This is a real honor and one that represents leadership, fellowship, friendship, trust, and compassion.

Each Princess and Chief, during the fall, winter, and spring, plans and composes the stunt for his or her Tribe. Princesses and Chiefs collect costumes and accessories, and write the lines to be rehearsed and directed when in Kamp. Judges selected are unbiased, perhaps guests, who have been invited for the Stunt Night by the Directors.

Stunt Nights were absolutely amazing events. All through the years – '30's, '40's, '50's, '60's, '70's and on – the Kampers, Princesses and Chiefs deserve a standing 'O'!

The Way We Were

The first two years Spike and I spent at Kanakuk Kamp are vivid in my "recall." Coach Lantz and his wife, Nell, lived in the office building. Spike spent nights as counselor in Cabin One, and Bill was a rookie Cabin Oner. Five-year-old Joe and I had a cabin just down the path toward the land where Kanakomo Kamp would eventually be established (circa 1958). Spike men hired Barney and Jane to join us in "running" the Kamp. Their daughter, Linda, was Joe's age and Russell, their son, was the age between Bill and Bob. It was an ideal and constructive summer for our families.

When Kanakomo was built, there was a fence already between the two Kamps. Although there was not a Gate, just an opening, Spike said the fence was electrified, and it served as a division of one Kamp from the other. Most everyone was gullible and believed it or "got the message!"

"Aunt Nell" Lantz and Darnell White

Barney Welch had played Varsity football at TAMU while Spike was on Faculty Staff in the Physical Ed/Athletic Programs. Barney was hired by the PE Department after his service in the Army of WWII. Spike, too, served USN on a carrier in the Pacific and returned to work in the P.E. Department as Head of Student Activities, including the Intramural Program. The Welch family fit in at Kamp. Jane and Linda shared the cabin with Joe and me. Spike and I soon afterwards lived in the back part of the office. Coach Lantz only came back on short visits to get his "Kanakuk Fix." He was enthusiastic and pleased to see the strides and activities Kanakuk Kamp was making.

I was learning so much those first couple of years: running out of staple groceries and needing supplies "yesterday!" and keeping books on any cash spent, paying payrolls, and following government demands. Fortunately, we had con-ferred with a CPA friend at home in Texas who outlined the necessity of keeping a log to record every transaction. Jane and I observed every detail and learned fast. Joe became a full-time Kamper at K-1 the second year we were at Kanakuk, and Linda, in 1958, was a charter Kamper of Kanakomo Kamp for Girls.

"Women don't belong in Kamp," was Coach Lantz's belief, "unless they are busy working to keep Kamp thriving. Nell Lantz, when she came with Coach Lantz in years past, often spent her summer living at the Branson Hotel. She was very fair-skinned and did not like to be in the sun and "outside." Meals for the "women" were served in the screened-in front part of the Office. I was wide-eyed and impressed that the Chiefs (Cherokee and Choctaw) delivered the food on trays. The Chiefs walked out the front door of Old Mess, across the path to the Office, and served the meal, then returned to take empty containers back to the kitchen. After Spike had a Kamp built for girls, it was so much better and natural: the girls shared the dining hall ("Old Mess") after the boys finished eating. Having girls around enhanced the whole atmosphere of kamping, although the girls had their own programs and schedules entirely on their premises, (unless boys' fields or Courts were vacant and available). The "bottom" on the lakeside for the girls had good tennis courts, as well as Tennis Courts on the hill across Lakeshore Drive. A good track was laid out for track meets, and a dock for canoes and ski boats was created. Sunday Evening Vespers for Kanakuk and Kanakomo were shared at Kanakomo Kamp's Church that overlooked the Lake. Dances and get-togethers at picnics were regularly shared Friday or Saturday night.

The girls were not the only ones who wore their finest shorts and "tees" when a get-together was scheduled. The girls would giggle and brush their hair with more interest. The boys didn't show their joy; however, it was easy to discern that they looked forward to the social events and "spiffed up" a bit, too. When Kanakomo was built, there was a fence already between the two Kamps. Although there was not a gate, just an opening, Spike said the fence was electrified, and it served as a division of one Kamp from the other. Most everyone was gullible and believed it or "got the message!"

Spike had a spacious and improved dining hall built several years after we purchased Kanakuk. The new dining hall was much appreciated by everyone. Conveniently, the girls entered from the northside, and the boys entered from the Southside. Girls always ate meals an hour after the boys. The Dining Hall was a popular and fun place for everyone. Birthdays were celebrated, and were "Big Deals".

Counselors' skits and gimmicks often opened the doors of laughter and celebrations. It was not unusual for a counselor to jump up on a bench and start singing his college/university song, and then have everyone else join in singing with him. Soon another would follow. Kanakomo counselors were entertaining and ingenuous with impromtu and delightful antics. Gail Guider took the prize when she led everyone in Mississippi State's theme song! The "Southern Gals" gave a significant "punch" to Kamp life. Counselors brought caps and banners, identifying their universities, to be hung in the dining hall. Spike was given caps from every college in the country, I think. Each counselor wanted Spike to wear his cap, so Spike wore different caps each day. Later, I began hanging them on rafters in my new office after Spike moved a Circa 1926 Cabin (renovated) for me in the vicinity of the Party Barn.

The "Remember Whens" are not forgotten.
"It just didn't get any better than that."

In the early years, at Taneycomo Court, Kampers and counselors sang camp songs daily. I don't remember when or why they stopped that wonderful singing. Kamp songbooks were distributed, and the typical and old camp songs with crazy verses were sung with laughter and fun. "Kum Bah Yah, My Lord" was never sung more inspiringly as the way the boys sounded when they sang. At the Girls' Kamp, the camp songs were sung with gusto often and spontaneously. Girls liked to sing!

At Final Ceremony, just as soon as the accolades and awards were presented and completed, the girls started singing their tear-jerker "Remember," and any hardhearted person who watched and listened to the girls pulled out a kleenex to wipe the tears. The girls sang with lots of tears flowing as they hugged their soon-to-be-departed friends at Kamp Kanakomo. It tugged on your emotions, big time!

The "Remember Whens" are not forgotten.
"It just didn't get any better than that."

The Slough Lady

It would be amiss to leave out the Slough Lady! No one talks about her anymore. Maybe she moved away since the slough was dredged out to make a lazy lagoon for Kampers in canoes.

Back when our family took the reigns at Kanakuk, new and younger Kampers were aware of the mysterious Slough Lady and wouldn't venture near the “slough” (a drainage and over-flow from the hills to the east running into Lake Taneycomo). “The Bottom” has always been a FUN and HAPPY place, especially after Rest Period in the hot summer months. Down by the lake it's many degrees cooler, and it is a haven for bird-watching and fishing. There are also fields and courts for badminton, softball, baseball, track, tennis, and the Ski Bug!

If I had been a kid, I would sure be scared to see the Slough Lady

Spike invented the Ski Bug which was a humongous donut with the center dug deep enough to hold water needed for skiing. He then rigged up a motor with steel arms reaching across the dry circle banks. The circling arms pulled the skier on skis so he could learn safely and easily to “stay on and not fall.” (Must have been worthy, it was used successfully for many years.)

After supper during Optional Period, many Kampers chose to go to the Bottom to fish in the “slough.” Along the secluded and pristine banks in the evening, the lazy shadows of the trees made a relaxing fisherman's paradise. A boy and his counselor bonded in the “not-a-care-in-the-world” setting, just fishin'! Occasionally, someone would interrupt a peaceful atmosphere and ask aloud, “Has anyone seen the Slough Lady lately? My Dad told me the Slough Lady lives here and roams around at night when we are asleep.”

There would always be the older Kampers who “had seen her last night” or “heard her outside their cabins.” If I had been a kid, I would sure be scared to see the Slough Lady! Anyway, I never saw her, not ever! Once, in later years, as I was walking down the lane to our house, a few straggler Kampers were scurrying back down to Kamp from Campbell Field where they had been playing soccer. They were taking a shortcut, across the rail fence and must have seen me. I heard one boy ask in a low voice, “Who is she? Is that the Slough Lady?”

I hadn't heard her name mentioned in years! Guess rumors never die!

"Hello, Sweet Darnell"

I am so excited that you (the matriarch!) are writing a book of memories! I can't wait to read it! I think anyone who attended Kamp when there was just plain old Kanakomo can relate to the excitement of going on a river trip with Spike loading us onto "Old Blue"! (Just like cattle.) We stood on duffle bags and hung over the sides of the truck singing (or for some of us - attempting to sing) along with "Mousie" until we had sung our repertoire many times over. Not just your everyday songs, mind you! Just the thought of flying through those Ozarks hills at what seemed to be 100 mph with the wind blowing through our hair and the sun shining down on us makes me chuckle! Now, once at the campsite, there was and never will be any experience similar to setting up a tent and awaiting inspection by Manley! I have no doubt that anyone ever just pitched her tent once only! Manley would shake it and walk around it until it collapsed! I believe this was close to being a ritual and rite of passage to being on the river for a week! Whether we returned to Kamp at the end of the trip with all our belongings or not, one thing is for sure, we returned thankful and happy for our accomplishments! Things were simple – just skipping a rock seemed like a major fete. And needless to say, jumping off bluffs into the water was as exciting as any amusement park ride could ever be.

K-K Guider

Forever ingrained in my memory is seeing Pardner paddling across freezing Lake Taneycomo in the early hours of the morning. As the fog was lifting, she happily placed a hand-picked flower on each and every table in the dining hall. Her beautiful flowers made everyday seem so special! She did this nearly to the end of her 100 years!

As a counselor, we were enabled with a sense of pride and knew that we had to deal with whatever came our way. I especially recall being on Table Rock Lake with Jim and Suzette Brawner and probably 30 plus 8-to-10 year olds. Our job was to teach all of the kids how to water ski. Sounds reasonable since we were spending a few nights camping and had a great ski boat! Somehow we accomplished this task even though our electric start on our boat malfunctioned; we taught all the kids by manually puffing the starter rope each and every time. It doesn't sound very challenging, but do you realize how many times a beginner skier falls only to stand on the skis 5 seconds? Somehow we survived and I will say, Jim, Suzette and I are probably stronger and better folks for being on that trip! There was such a hardworking and honest work ethic that was passed on to all of us.

I always laugh about the time Debbie Jo and I were out sailing on Table Rock Lake. Debbie Jo was so cute and had a mouth full of braces. As careful as we were in the water and always with a buddy, never did I expect for her to get tangled up with her life jacket while we were laughing. To this day, I don't know how she did it, but she caught her big orange life jacket on her front braces! Thank goodness, she is still with us today! It was not a pretty sight! These silly times sound kind of dumb, but I can't tell you how we laughed and laughed at crazy things like this.

The "Ponytail Parthenon" was better than NYC and any production at Kanakomo could have rivaled Broadway in a second. With original scripts, buckets of tempera paint and cardboard boxes, we sure witnessed some entertainment in the cool mountain air! The costume box seemed to have an endless array of outfits for every occasion imaginable. Lovely hats and formals seemed to fit anyone, anytime, and for any occasion. The excitement that filled the air on Opening Day of the production was so exhilarating.

Way before VHS tapes and DVD's, Spike and Darnell visited our family and showed the Kamp Films in our town, Vicksburg, MS. This was more special than if the King and Queen were visiting! They brought such love and joy to everyone. They were energetic and worked hard travelling to so many states, hauling their projector and equipment. What a wonderful place they created for all of us and our kids and grandkids!

A very special time at Kamp was spending a "Dimies!" Enough said! This rivaled Swim Meets, Canoe Meets (my favorite: "Ins" and "Outs" in the coldest water on earth!), and Track Meets. Nothing, however, compared to Sunday mornings and Spike's I'M THIRD" Sermon. Sunday mornings and Evening Vespers shaped so many of us into the adults we are today. I have no doubt about that.

Well, I could ramble on forever. Good luck with the book. I can't wait to read it.

Love,

K-K Guider Jacobs

Kanakomo 1965-74

In 1965, I attended first term at Kanakomo Kamp in Branson, Missouri. At the end of those five weeks, I was a different person. It has had a defining influence ever since. Forty years later the memories and experiences are as vivid as if they happened yesterday.

As I walked through the gates that bright June morning, I was immediately awed by what I saw. The facilities were amazing – in-ground trampolines, ping pong tables, a gym, something called the Ponytale Parthenon and cabin after cabin – all on a bluff overlooking Lake Taneycomo. In a matter of hours, I would see every athletic field and facility imaginable. I was in heaven!

I was assigned to Cabin 6 and my counselor was Susan Farrar. She exemplified the people I would meet and the lifelong relationships I would develop during my 8 years at Kamp. She was bright, funny, kind and athletic. Susan was larger than life as were so many I would meet that summer.

It wasn't long before I saw what "larger than life" really meant. I met Spike and Darnell White, the owners of Kanakuk Kamp for Boys and Kanakomo Kamp for Girls. They had it all before we even knew what having it all meant – a great marriage, three handsome sons, their very own camp and a love and respect for everyone. It set the tone for the camp at that time and their influence and vision continues to this day.

The amazing people just kept coming – Manley and Lenna Vance, Kanakomo's first directors; Judy Booth, head counselor; Debbie-Jo White, also a director; and a multitude of senior and junior counselors. In my mind, the staff seemed to exist so that I could have fun. It was unlike anything I had ever experienced.

And my fellow Kampers: I'd met a group of friends who were interested in friendly competition, learning new skills, and having a great time.

I was a Kickapoo and thrived on the competition with the Kiowas. And did we ever compete! We earned points playing softball, running track, at riflery and archery, throwing darts, and much more. Even better than the daily competition were the 6 meets we had during the term – two each in swimming, track and canoe. These events were a tremendous learning experience both as a Kamper and as a staff member. We learned to organize, manage and work under deadline. It was intoxicating.

So many memories:

Tribal Stunts

Each tribe worked on an original play throughout the term. Near the end of Kamp, it was performed for the opposing tribe and the guys at Kanakuk. The stunt judged as the best received points. At Kanakomo we competed even in drama.

Trips

There were three-day float trips on the Buffalo, White and Current Rivers.

The most memorable float trip, maybe in the history of Kanakomo, was in 1967 when the Buffalo flooded and the Kickapoos had to spend the night at Boy Scout Camp Orr.

The Truck Trip – three days riding around Southwest Missouri and Northwest Arkansas making memories.

All trips ended with the distribution of "dimies" –

usually two dimes we were allowed to spend on the treat of our choice, most often ice cream.

Big and Little K's

Earning a Big or Little K signified proficiency in the sports and activities learned at Kamp.

Sunday sermons

Most memorable were those delivered by Spike; talks that were "on the bottom shelf," accessible on all age levels and unforgettable in their message. They included I'm Third, A Rock at a Time and Four Square Life.

End of Kamp award ceremony

Kampers received ribbons for placing in the final swim and track meets, patches for achieving proficiency in riflery and swimming, and trophies for honor Kamper in the three age divisions. But to this day, the neatest award I have ever seen were the painted miniature paddles presented to the Honor Trippers.

Skiing

Learning to ski on the "Ski Bug" and then behind a boat in the frigid water of Lake Taneycomo.

Kanakuk

Once-a-term dances and "Kanakuk Goodies"

Ceramics
- Ann Schantz

Miss-A-Meal

Going without lunch on the next-to-last day of kamp with the money saved going to hunger relief. For me, it was my first exposure to sacrifical giving.

Kamp Championships

Competitions in sports like washers, tether ball and aerial darts were held the last week of Kamp. Ribbons were awarded to the champion and runner-up and points to the winning tribe.

Princesses and Squaws

Kamper and staff leaders of the tribes. Original role models for many.

Singing

We sang, or were sung to, constantly. I can still remember the words to many of the songs.

The food

There was Kamp Koffee Kake for breakfast and fried chicken for lunch on Sundays. A letter home was required for admittance to the dining hall, and served with "never-empty pitchers of cold, pasteurized milk."

The Komo Katch-Up, yearbook and movies

These were part of our winter routine and were eagerly awaited. The Katch-Up newsletter was designed to help Kampers stay in touch; the yearbook served as the historical record of the summer and the movies shown in your very own hometown and starring you!

Staff duties

The worst being pulling day lily stems between first and second terms.

Because of my love of all things Kanakuk and Kanakomo, I became enamored with the history of the camps. I turned this interest into "History of Kanakomo" -- moments delivered following rest period each day. A favorite was "Uncle Bill, Uncle Bob and Uncle Tom, and How to Tell the Difference."

Sometimes after a church retreat, a weekend trip with friends, or an activity which spans a number of days, I find myself thinking that I feel like I've been to camp. That is high praise and is a feeling that is a result of my time at Kanakomo. So many good things relate back to a time when it seemed I didn't have a care in the world. It was a time when my faith developed. It was a time when I learned life-long skills and made lasting friends. What a gift it was. What a gift it still is.

Robert Calden "Uncle Bob"

After Jane Brockman had been a Kamper for many summers and on Staff, one of her "specialties" (there were many and she was a "pro" advocator of Kamp traditions and history) was "UNCLES and WHO-IS-WHO and WHEN-AND-WHY." Soon after new Kampers arrived and were adapting to schedules and locations and awed by the hyped enthusiasm of their counselors, Jane would stand on the stage of Ponytail Parthenon to lecture on the "Uncles" of KUK and KOMO.

She told the story of Kanakuk and Kanakomo and "Uncle Bob" and "Uncle Bill " and "Pardner, the Flower Lady." The little girls on the first row were wide-eyed, restless, and fidgety, ready to go play, and the bigger girls were enraptured more by Jane Brockman, the story teller, than the folks she talked about. Jane put the capital on Fun and Wonder and Kamp! (I would like her version and insight right now as I include "Uncle Bob" to the Patches of the Past.

When we purchased Kanakuk Kamp, we inherited a treasure: Robert Calden. He was a gentle gentleman, well-educated, reserved and respected for his loyalty and dedication to Kanakuk's upkeep and the worthiness of Kanakuk's Aims and Goal. He lived and worked at Kanakuk year 'round.

He was 71 years of age when "Uncle Bill" heard about a man across the Lake on the opposite hill who had been caring for an elderly man who had died. Uncle Bill called on Bob Calden with the purpose of hiring him to be the caretaker and live at Kamp Kanakuk.

Robert Calden was a native of Norway and came to the United States to work for Tiffany's in New York City. How he ended up on a forlorn hill on the outskirts of the city limits of Branson is a mystery to me. Perhaps it was the home of the elderly man he had known in New York.

The Kampers dubbed him "Uncle Bob." He subscribed to the New York Times, the Wall Street Journal, and read good literature. Nell Lantz gave him books to read in the wintertime, and I shared books with him, too. He was gracious and retiring, almost like a nymph, not seen too much, working with flowers, repairing canoes, tending to chores. He was a sweet spirited and hospitable little man. He and Spike were fine friends and he often said to Spike, "Best Kamp in the Country, Spike!"

He was proud of every improvement and addition Spike accomplished. When the Girls' Kamp was built, Bob's cabin was slightly beyond the path that the girls traveled three times a day, to the dining hall (shared with the boys at another schedule). Every evening at the time the girls came down the path, Uncle Bob was sitting in his rocking chair, waiting to be greeted by the girls: "Hi, Uncle Bob!". In turn, in his European manner, he would bow, smile, nod, and wave his hand. That was definitely the "best-of-the-day" for Uncle Bob. His shy and sharing personality was infectious. Often in the evening when it was too hot and humid to be indoors, Jane and I would sit in two chairs outside the office. It was a pleasant place in the shade and because Uncle Bob (without our knowing or seeing him) had sprinkled the gravel path and around the area to cool the atmosphere for us. Often he would leave his daily newspaper folded neatly at the front door – just like the story-book "fairies."

The best memories of Uncle Bob were at the Council Ring when the Indians were dancing and the ceremonies were performed. It was a solemn affair, and my office girls were always curious and wanting to see it, too. One time each summer I snuck the girls up through the woods, over the rail fence, and hoped Spike didn't see or hear us. The girls tucked their hair under a cap to look like the Kampers. We softly approached the Ring going from one big tree and advancing to another until close enough to see the show. One time, as I made my way to a tree to hide behind, I practically ran into Uncle Bob doing the same thing. I grinned at him in the dark, patted him on the back and advanced to another tree.

"Big Deal"

Everything's a "big deal" at Kanakuk Kamps. Spike made a big deal out of the seemingly smallest occasions. The overweight boys whose parents thought that they might lose weight at Kanakuk through the exercise and sports were made to feel comfortable and not different. Their cabin mates and counselors were "friends" and were pulling for them. Those boys wanted very much to trim down in order to participate in activities at Kamp and later at school, where they felt "left out" of a lot of games. Losing weight was "fun" for the boys at Kamp. Everyone was a cheerleader, and All-Kamp made a "big deal" when the boys trimmed up. Barney Welch kept a few Hershey bars in the "frig" in the back of Old Mess (just for the Kampers who individually asked to lose weight) to be presented at the Final Awards Ceremony. Much "ado" was made to encourage and make the sacrifice a "big deal." Those kampers trimmed up and became strong just because of the activities and "three-meals-a-day with no snacks" and automatically lost weight. They returned home with better self-images. They deserved a very BIG DEAL!

Birthdays for Kampers during the 7-weeks Term were celebrated with a "big-deal-fanfare." Kampers never felt "cheated" about not being home where school friends came over for cake and ice cream. At the Noon meal, counselors joined in "raps" and parades, beating on pots and pans while (despite the raised eyebrows and frowns of the cooks) singing and weaving in and around the tables, stopping in front of the "birthday boy or birthday girl." I probably was not the only person who envied those having a birthday in June, July, or August at Kamp.

For several years the Fatheree family from west Texas had two sets of twins at the Kamps. One set: Sarah and Tim, and second set: Matt and Millie. More astounding: the two sets were born on the same day (different years). That was the only time each Kamp had two boys and two girls celebrating at each Kamp's "Big Deal." What are the odds that this could happen to ANY camp?

Other celebrations were held for various accomplishments. Swimming across the pool for the first time and jumping off the diving board both were "big deals." Everyone and everything at Kamp was a "big deal." It wasn't just about Blue Ribbon and Medal Winners, Beauty Contests, or Super Studs. Each Kamper was special at Kanakuk. Today, "Big Deals" are excitedly and enthusiastically doled out to all Kampers with meaning and sincerity. Often it doesn't take much more than a pat-on-the-back, some applause, or an ear to listen – really listen – and understand to make a Kamper feel important.

Kamp Vespers

The Boys' Kamp joined the Girls' Kamp Sunday evenings at dusk. The setting at Kanakomo Kamp Church was special for everyone. Vespers had a glow that lit up an ordinary program. Sitting there at church, looking out on Lake Taneycomo below, with the moon shining made an auspicious and spectacular site "Unto these hills."

Spike usually had a "big deal" planned for Vespers and the experience was always memorable for young and old alike. Two particular presentations, LET YOU LIGHT SO SHINE and ONE STEP AT A TIME, were awesome and distinctly effective for everyone. One particular Vespers service had an after-effect that two work boys doubtlessly remember. Spike had planned a little drama to be coordinated with his TALK. The two work boys were to be directed at a specific time on the shore next to the lake below. However, as in a line of a poem by Robert Burn, "Best laid plans, oft gone awry," the two leading "actors" in Spike's plan made a few alterations to the script. According to Spike's scenario, two canoes would be paddled silently across the lake. Each canoe would carry one work boy holding a lighted torch, drop off the boys ashore on opposite side, then paddle back to Kamp's beach. The two work boys, in the meantime, would light one of the many prepared piles, each pile made up of twigs, dead leaves, and wood shavings, and each spread apart, down a long line – spreading the Light!

It all sounded like a Standing-Room-Only performance!

However, unbeknownst to Spike, the "stage-hands" had previously poured kerosene on every pile a few hours before. Instead of an inspirational and far-away effect of fading fires and fairy-tale lights, there appeared exploding, blazing bonfires, one after another. It was more like an illustration of "Fire and Brimstone!" It was told later that the actors were running for their own safety as each torch hit the pile and exploded! As a driver was designated to pick the two work boys up at a road nearby, the two culprits arrived unscathed, snickering and laughing.

There stood Spike! . . . . . Enough said!

"Hello Mudder, Hello Fadder"

Members of C.A.M.P. (Texas Private Camps for Youth) were meeting in Austin to discuss and attend seminars to learn and exchange ideas and experiences. "Tex" Robertson, founder and owner of Camp LONGHORN (and a good friend of Spike's), was the Head Honcho conducting an open forum, so to speak.

There were many questions and discussions about "letters written to parents during the term their campers were at Camp". Everyone gave suggestions. One Director asked, "What do you advise when a counselor has a camper who is a bully, who complains, and who causes disruption to the Cabin's otherwise compatible and neat kids? Do you recommend that the Counselor write to this camper's parents about their undisciplined kid's selfish and belligerent attitude?"

There was a lot of laughter and crazy answers thrown out in the room. Every Director and Camp Owner understood the dilemma. Spike was grinning and asked, "Tex, how do you handle that?" Tex smiled and said, "Well, at Camp Longhorn, we just write to the parents and say, "Your son is having a blast at camp. He is a pretty good kid."

At Kanakuk Kamp, Spike had his own formula. Each Counselor was given a card that had several "one-liners" and subjects to write about to the parents of each Kamper in his cabin. The letters were then turned in at the Office. The office girls and I would read each letter to correct terrible punctuation and misspelled words (didn't want the parents to judge the counselor by his poor grammar and spelling). If needed, the letter would be returned and rewritten. There were several letters each term written about "a pretty good boy."

Conversely, the Kampers wrote letters to their parents. Every Sunday before dismissal, the Kampers were told to go back to their cabins and write a letter to their parents. That letter would be their pass to enter the Dining Hall for Sunday Fried Chicken! That cinched it two ways: 1. No one in his right mind would want to miss fried chicken at Kanakuk Kamps! And 2. At least one letter a week was sent to the Parents!

Often parents would write to Kamp and send a copy of their son or daughters letter to share with us something funny or complimentary about Kamp.

One such letter was written by a Jewish boy named Ira:

"Dear Mother and Dad,

Today is Sunday. You know what that is. Don't worry, when they say 'Jesus', I say 'God" instead. I am having fun, Love, Ira

Incidentally, at an American Camping Association Conference we attended, the man who wrote the lyrics and music to "Hello, Mudder, Hello, Fadder" was a guest performer. Camp members and attendants applauded and called for him to "sing it again." That song was popular and sung all over the country in camps when the song was still Top Ten.

July 4 , 1953

Dear Dr. and Mrs. Baldwin,

It is really a pleasure to have such a fine boy as Dick in my cabin. He is a perfect gentleman in every respect. He gets along fine with the other boys and does his job well in the cabin.

He is well and as happy as can be, – enjoying camp to the fullest. I don't believe he has gained any weight nor has he lost any. His appetite is fine and he eats everything.

Competition among the tribes is keen. First Choctaws ahead and then the Cherokees. The Choctaws won the stunt, but the Cherokees came back winning the swimming and track meets. The intermediate division is plenty good, and Dick got his share of points in both swimming and track. He has passed a number of his "K" tests.

If there is any one thing you wish Dick to gain from his camp experience this summer, please let me know and I will do my best to see that he gets it.

Hope you are having a pleasant summer.

Your son's counselor

Floyd Rutherford

Bob, Bill, and Joe

All the time Bob, Bill, and Joe were growing up, Spike and I remained in College Station. Spike continued to work at Texas A&M nine months of the year until the two Kamps grew in enrollment and size.

It was wonderful when Spike finally got to give full-time attention to the operation of Kanakuk Kamps. Spike had a talent for envisioning "fun-for-kids" game apparatuses and then building them. As a boy he built a zipline and slides, tree houses, and anything for adventure and fun. Kids in the neighborhood were usually where Spike was - trying out and having fun on his new inventions.

As a Director of Youth Kamps, he built Zip Lines, Tree-Top adventures, mud slides, ponds for the Blob, Pools, towers for diving into the lake, and sports games. Spike was in his element! Every weird and exciting new "play thing" he built, he tried out first. (It was a "given" that his sons did, too!). IF

> It seemed that not one of our sons wanted to join us at Kanakuk as a career.

it proved safe for our sons, then he opened it for the Kampers. Spike was a graduate engineer from TAMU; that education and Spike's inventive mind were assets for a Youth Camp.

Above: Bob White.
Below: Bill White.
Lower Left: Joe White

After "kamper-age," Bob graduated from SMU where he was on the Varsity Swim Team under Coach Red Barr. He then graduated from Baylor Dental College. Bill attended SMU, where he played football. After concussion, however, the doctors advised that Bill not play football again. Bill then chose to return to College Station and get his Degree at Texas A&M, much to the pleasure of Spike. Two Aggies in the home was enough!

Joe, in the meantime, had a pre-med destination. It seemed that not one of our sons wanted to join us at Kanakuk! However, at the end of Joe's Junior year at SMU, he told Spike and me that he wanted to be a part of Kamp permanently. We were ecstatic and felt blessed for Joe's decision. Bill said, "We knew one of us had to run Kamp someday, and I knew it wouldn't be me." Jokingly, we laughed and said, "We knew it wouldn't be Bill, either!" Actually, Bob and Bill were pleased and had faith that Joe would be the perfect heir to further the goals for Kanakuk.

“Spike-isms”

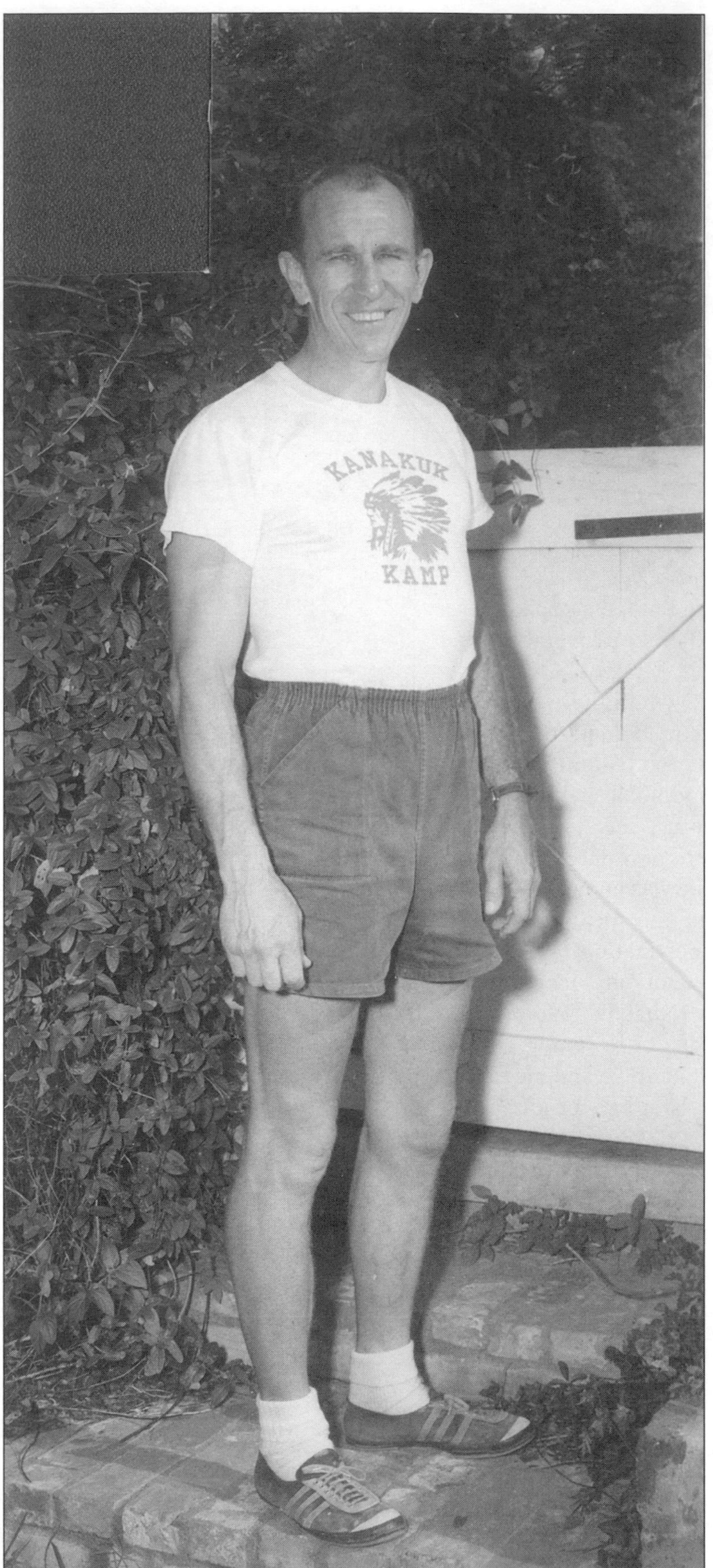

Spike had innumerable “sayings” that we all picked up and quoted. After he died, Debbie Jo said, “We need to recall and write down all his quips and keep a list of them.” Tex Robertson of Camp Longhorn in the Texas “Hill Country” was a great friend of Spike’s and dubbed the sayings “Spike-isms.” Tex sent a card to Spike a few days before he died, which was the day Kanakuk Kamps opened. He wrote: “Hey, Spike, Camp Longhorn is soon to open, and we haven’t had our “Spike-ism” for the summer yet. Send muy pronto. TEX”

Every one of us who worked with Spike learned to be enthusiastic and go with the flow.

The “ten minute job” was a saying used frequently. I cringed whenever I heard Spike giving me or anyone else a job to do that he introduced as a “ten minute job!” It might take a couple of hours, at least. Spike had a flare for making every chore or project you were given as if you were really hand-selected and fortunate and to be the recipient of the job. Every one of us who worked with Spike learned to be enthusiastic and go with the flow. You couldn’t tell him, “No deal.” Somehow he would go out one door and come back through another, and you would find yourself doing the job with fervor.

“You don’t have to, you get to” was a classic “Spike-ism.” Spike made us believe it was a privilege to be active and involved. You just couldn’t win “your way.” It could be a foggy dreary, dull day, but Spike’s jaunty “It’s a beautiful day in the Ozarks” would chase the clouds away.

Spike had a caption for every occasion, and Joe is just like him. He has the same attitude and dedication. – Everything is a “Big Deal.” Encouragement and enthusiasm accompany the simplest or the most difficult projects. Try as you might, you will find yourself believing and joining up as if it were “your” goal. Every summer one of the “isms” would be the popularly repeated saying that caught on by everyone.

More "Spike-isms"

I recall the long, long trek driving back to College Station after Kamp was over. I drove the Kamp Station Wagon, loaded with Office Records, personal gear, plus the boys until they were College students and traveled on their own. As I headed out the gate, I said, "It's a long trip and I dread it." Spike said, "It's only long if you think it is." I muttered bravely, "I think it is!"

These are some of the "ism's" that I recall:

"WHEN ONE WORKS, EVERYBODY WORKS"

"IT'S BETTER THAN NEW, IT'S BEEN USED"

"YOU'LL BE BETTER WIVES AND BETTER MOTHERS"

"DARNELL, NOW LISTEN"
"THAT'S DUMB!"

"IT'S NOT DIFFICULT UNLESS YOU THINK IT IS"

"WHEN THINGS GET TOUGH, KNEEL"

"DON'T GO EMPTY-HANDED"

"IT'S A BEAUTIFUL DAY IN THE OZARKS"
(Even if the day was dreary, dull, and dripping wet!)

"GOD DON'T MAKE NO JUNK!"

"WHEN YOU TALK TO SOMEONE, LOOK HIM IN THE EYE"

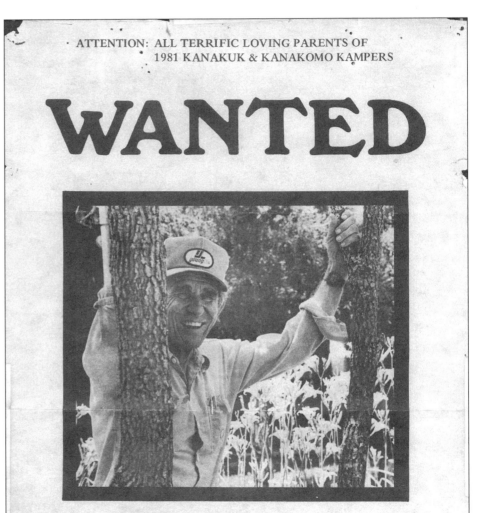

ATTENTION: ALL TERRIFIC LOVING PARENTS OF
1981 KANAKUK & KANAKOMO KAMPERS

WANTED

SPIKE WHITE

$1,000,000 REWARD

* This man was last seen with his family and gang members trying desperately to say Thank You with letters, phone calls, hugs and smiles to all the "Just-a-Parents" of the kids of Kanakuk and Kanakomo.

* He can be recognized by a twinkle in his eye, a kind happy face and the words "Thank You Moms and Dads" coming out of his mouth.

* Be careful. He is dangerous. He may hug you tightly and brighten your day like it's never been

Paddlin' With Spike

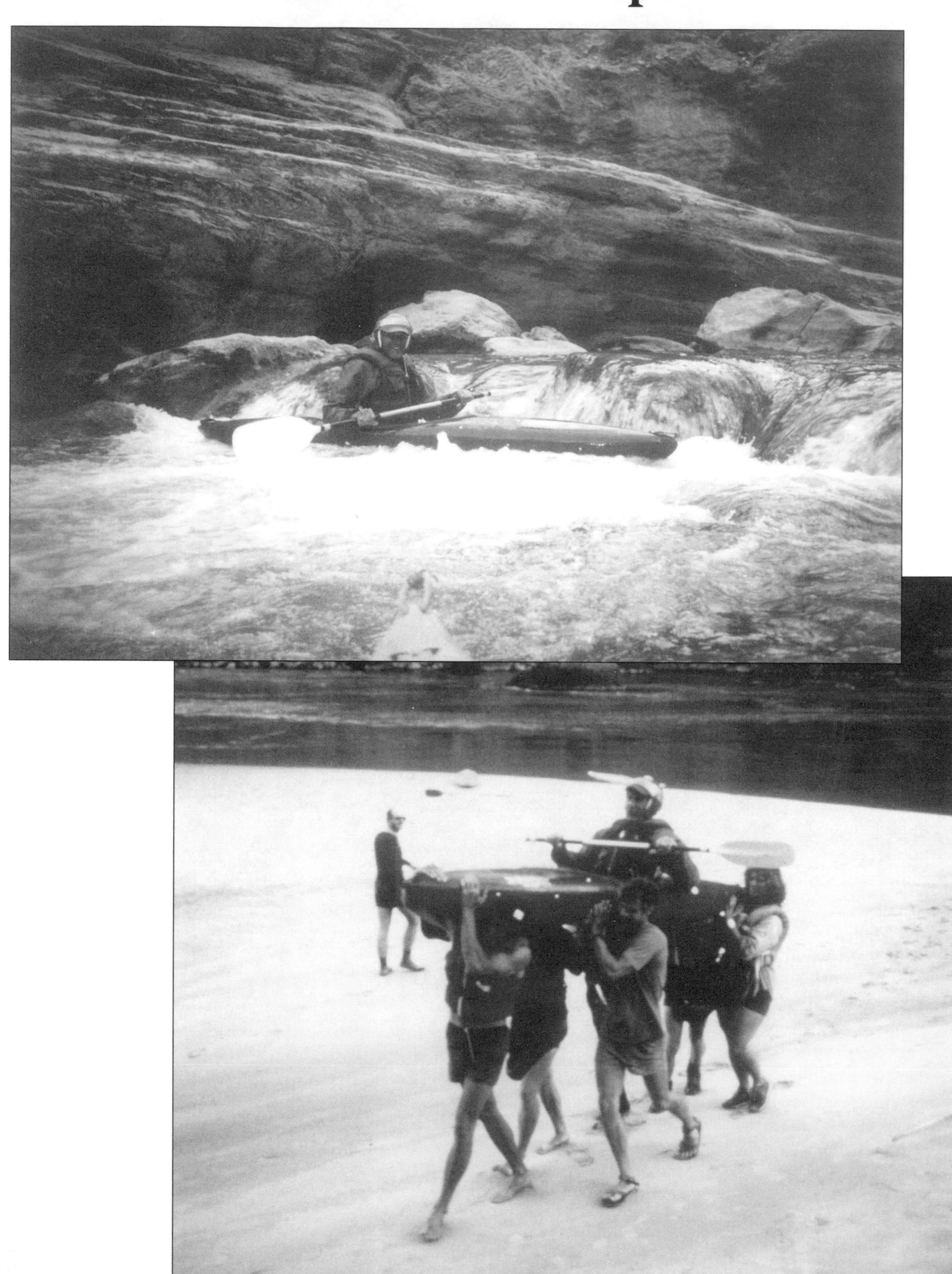

Spike, His Dog and His Red Truck

Spike had a great connection with each of his Labs. There's a game called 20 Questions. Usually, someone sneaks in being an animal to confuse the game. If I chose an animal, I would pick, "Spike's Labrador Retriever!" A dog of Spike's went everywhere with him and would sit like a King on a throne on top of the tool chest just behind Spike's truck seat – the dog would travel down a road or through the woods or down by the lake with the soft cooling breezes blowing in his face, watching and smelling all the woods, farms, roads, and waters they passed – just riding with Spike! His last dog, "Tex," and Spike argued at each other like two humans. As the two of them sped down the highway, Spike would yell out the window to Tex, "Tex, SIT DOWN!" Tex would bark loudly back! That would go on until the car stopped at its destination.

"It just gets dirty again." He would say, "The truck works for me; I don't work for the truck."

Once, when I was waiting for my car to be checked in order to get a license renewal, a man who was also waiting (probably had heard the serviceman call me "Mrs. White,") asked, "Are you any kin to that man who drives the red truck with the dog riding on the tool chest?" As soon as I was hearing this, I knew without further words the man was going to upbraid Spike for letting that dog ride precariously on the top of the tool chest (I had had that asked by a few people before. I sweetly responded, "Yes, that's Spike White; he is my husband." The man sourly said, "That's the dirtiest pick-up I have ever seen." The man was right, to be sure. Spike worked on rough grounds, constructing Kamps with pools, cabins, athletic fields in all kinds of weather: heat, humidity, cold, snow, rain and sleet, and his car stayed "dirty." I washed my own car and took pride in keeping it clean and occasionally washed Spike's when he wasn't around. He did not like for me to spend my energy on the truck. His philosophy: "It just gets dirty again." He would say, "The truck works for me; I don't work for the truck." That made sense!

It was really kinda' fun to hear our sons and other friends (many did) "ride" Spike about his truck with its dents from backing into trees or dumps of debris or loads of lumber. If you ever sat in front, you forgot about the unimportant things on the outside. Spike's truck was a happy truck. As soon as the key turned on the ignition, music would be playing: cassettes of Dan Roberts singing many of Spike's favorite songs: "Just A Closer Walk With Thee," 'It Is No Secret What God Can Do," Dallas Holmes, Cowboy Songs, Willie Nelson and others. Spike would join in and enjoy!

Spike liked talking, listening, and visiting with everyone he encountered. Usually he had a story to tell me at the Opening or Closing of Kamp about parents he had encountered when he was driving through Kamp. One dad was walking up the rough, narrow, steep, and winding road to the top, and Spike, stopped to ask if he wanted to ride. Spike greeted him, and the man asked what kind of work he did at Kamp. Spike answered, "Oh, I just mostly pick up trash and odd jobs." You didn't work FOR Spike; you worked WITH him.

I was amused and later thought, "Wonder what the man thought that next day, at the Final Ceremony, when he saw Spike in front speaking and handing out awards."

Spike had a healthy self-esteem and never needed accolades. He enjoyed applauding, encouraging, listening, and serving. He liked to see others being praised and rewarded. He never took affront when people treated him differently because they thought he was a hired hand because he never felt that there was a difference, and there shouldn't be!

Another time when parents were at Kamp for the Meets and Ceremonies, Spike stopped to give a ride to a man. Spike asked him who he was, and the man answered, "I'm just a parent." Spike and I talked about those words, and I wrote a poem to give to Spike. He liked it very much and insisted that I let him read it at Final Ceremonies.

JUST A PARENT

To the searching world of Science, Space, and Such -
My role on earth may not appear to amount to much –
I can't boast of Big Corporation schemes of success –
Nor list great accomplishments in one column or less –
Walters wouldn't televise a Talk Show, not with me –
Very few merits her newsworthy mind could even see –
Time spent on the Universe reveals little, if it at all –
I'm JUST A PARENT – one of many that pass each day –
What we do may seem insignificant – just "by the way" –
JUST A PARENT whose aim is to create a home of love –
Not capable alone but gets direction from the One Above –
Serving, sharing, caring –giving up and giving out –
Playing, paying, praying –having faith, having doubt –
Trying, denying, crying – years of love and celebrations –
JUST A PARENT with dreams for children we beget –
Aspiring for their future – much bigger and better, YET –
Pleading, leading – for the paths of Truth and of Light –
Teaching, reaching – for the spectrum of Greater Height.

"The Flower Lady"

My mother, after our second son, Bob, was born, was asked, "What will little Bob call you?" Without any hesitation, she quickly answered, "Pardner!" She was East Texas born and a cowgirl at heart. As a girl she had her own pony to ride to school (and her siblings walked). As an adult living in Dallas, she owned a Quarter Horse name "Poncho."

Pardner rode in parades with friends with the same equestrian interests. Their horses were trained to dance the lively Square Dance. The owners were dressed in spectacular manner. Her grandchildren and greatgrandchildren continued to call her "Pardner," and it fit her well. She had an effervescence, an optimistic vitality, a "true grit" and an "ain't-down-yet" personality, Texas-style! Nothing defeated her – not trouble, trials, or tribulations. Her siblings were ten in number, and Pardner let the brothers and sisters know that she was "Papa's Pet" (as if they didn't already know it!) Her childhood life would make an interesting and captivating book to read. Pardner's "rest-of-her-story" life has enchanted and entertained those of us who have shared that part of life with her major influence and genes that run strongly through our progeny.

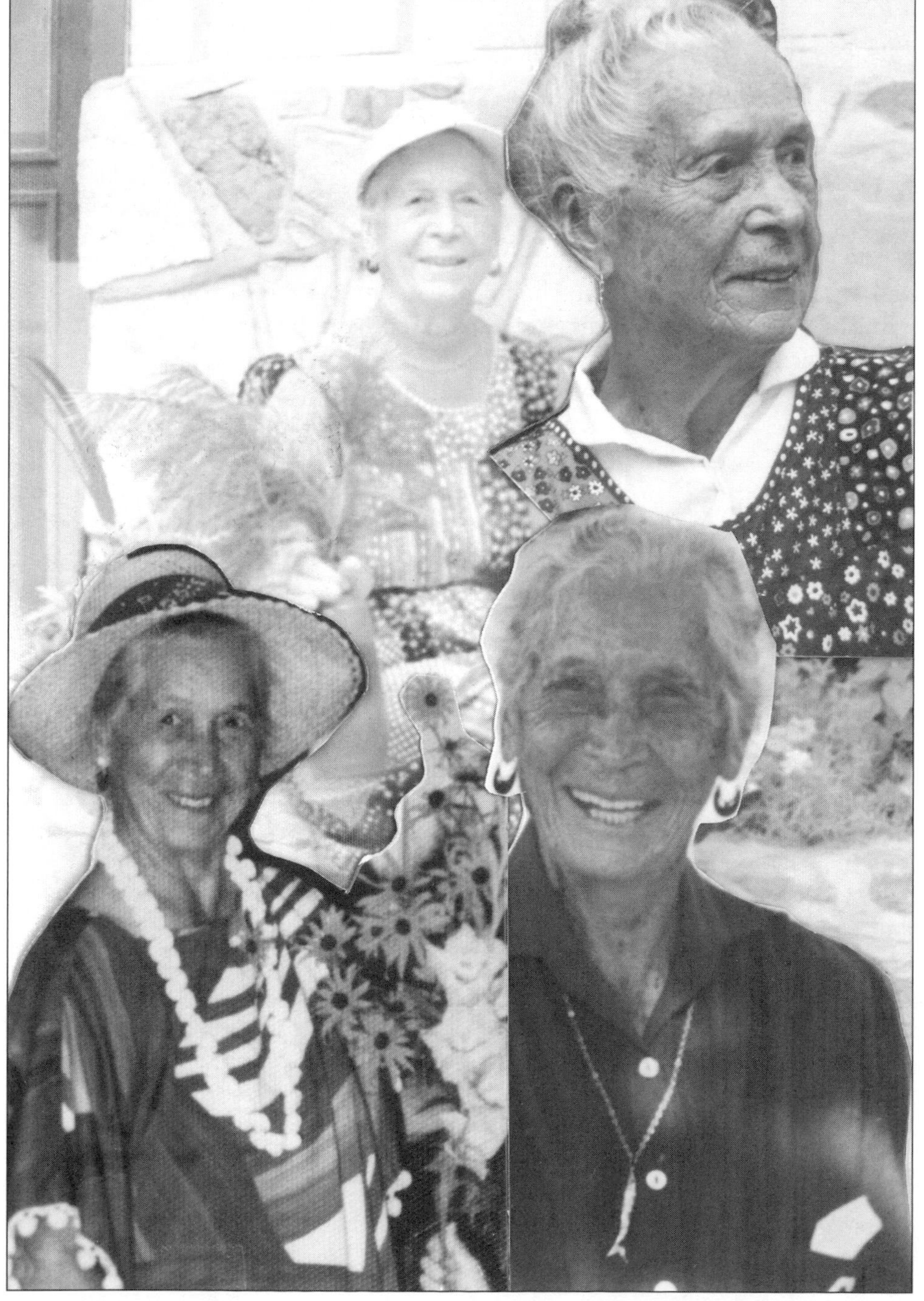

Pardner visited Kanakuk Kamp occasionally after we purchased the Kamp, but she did not take part in it until our sons were high school age and older. She had built her own cabin in order to be independent and fill a niche that she discovered was needed. One side of Pardner's cabin was offered and hastily accepted by Cliff and Lib Ackerman, very fine, steller, key Staff members for Kanakomo and Kanakuk. Uncle Bob, our year-round Caretaker, had planted and tended the flowers for years until it became too hard for him. Pardner took over. Her energetic love for flowers made a remarkable difference on the Kamp grounds.

When Joe graduated from SMU, we made the decision to move permanently to Kanakuk. Spike invited Pardner to move to Branson with us.

Pardner was akin to a nomad. Picking up and pitching a "tent" was a new adventure with new horizons to conquer for Pardner. Pardner, independently, without any fanfare, purchased a house in a new development directly across the Lake from Kanakuk. She was settled before Spike and I arrived a few weeks later. She also had purchased a boat and motor, gone fishing daily, and had made friends with good neighbors (mostly retired). She wanted to get out of the big cities and "go fishin'" every day. Pardner had arrived and let her anchor down in Branson, Missouri, just eight arrow-flights from Kanakuk Kamp.

Every morning before Reveille, Pardner motored across the foggy lake, docked her boat at Kanakuk's dock, walked across the field, made her way up the many steps to the top, and dropped in the Kitchen to say, "Good Morning" to the cooks. She would then start to tend her flower beds. During the morning she was spading the beds of plants, planting more, and cutting blooms for the "sick kids" and nurses at the hospital. Often, I regret she did not wear a pedometer. That dear little lady must have walked miles each day, all over the grounds and mostly in the woods and out-of-the-mowed-and smooth playing fields. She transplanted beautiful, native plants that enhanced the Kamp grounds at both Kamps. She pulled up poison ivy with her bare hands, thus keeping the Kamp free of the rash and pain it caused a Kamper.

The Kanakomo Kampers gave her the name "The Flower Lady." Pardner had a style of dress that fit her personality: colorful, bizarre, bright, and happy. She called everyone "Dahlin'" (not bothered to know anyone's real name). She was like an enchanting character in the best book you've ever read, over again and again. Her winsome ways captured the hearts of little Kampers, teenagers, and Staff . She wasn't partial to any one, certainly not any celebrity, king, or president. In a short time, she could change a messed-up hippy or hoodlum into a decent and self-respected person. If you ever met her, you were caught up with her East Texas humor and philosophy, and you wanted more. She was like a magnet that drew you closer. Kampers, both boys and girls, yearned to go along with her as she wandered off the beaten paths. She was a Pied Piper. No one of us could get enough of her magnetic warmth and the tall Texas tales she could weave. The Girls' Kamp had a fountain built at their church and dedicated it to their loved "Pardner, The Flower Lady." The neatest thing about that: it was built and dedicated to her when she was still active and working. Many children, later grown and having second and third generations at Kamp, have reminisced and expressed their love and admiration for Pardner. She is not forgotten! Her indelible impression remains on these grounds and in the hearts of all of us.

When Pardner moved to Branson, she also removed her monument from the cemetery in Dallas. My brother was buried there. My mother had purchased two other plots where she planned to be buried someday and one for me, if needed someday. Pardner's monument had only her name and the year of her birth: 1894 (and the "dash" to be added). Being practical and foreseeing that it would be right to be buried with Spike and me at the Kamp Cemetery, she simplified it down the line of time to have that contingency taken care of! We really didn't know that she had done until later.

[After 25 or more years of working at the regular and original Office at Kanakuk, Spike said, “Darnell, there is an old cabin (circa 1926) that needs to be either torn down or moved. It would be a great private office for you.” It was exciting to watch the renovation in that wonderful spot. I personally have glorious memories: Kanakomo kampers passing by, coming and going to activities, and always calling out in unison: “Hi, Darnell!” I was privileged to teach nature classes to the girls: wild flowers on nature hikes, Sun-Art photography and Nature Art projects outside in the yard were enjoyed That dear cabin/office?? filled my cup to overflowing. Watching the Kampers and hearing the happy voices and laughter all day made the years of work worthwhile and rewarding.]

Pardner planted native shrubs and beautified the little yard surrounded by a rail fence in front of the Office-Cabin. I had the pleasure of seeing her and visiting with her during the days. Just as Pardner daily brought cut flowers to take to Kampers confined in the Kamp hospital, she always brought a bouquet to me for my Office. Pardner usually had some teenage boy following her around carrying buckets or baskets of plants while also following her directions and listening to her stories. Pardner had a natural discernment and acumen in sizing up people and their need.

Pardner's sincere respect and love for young, old, all races and color was amazing. During Work Week when everyone was grouped and working Pardner would ask the Head Counselor or Director, “Do you have anyone who doesn't know HOW to work, and you don't know what to do with?” She was the one person who could teach, train and convert a person to enjoy and revel in the lessons learned under the guidance, enthusiasm and faith shown by that little Texas lady.

In my office one morning I could hear Pardner talking to a young man as they were chopping and pulling up weeds. The “Rookie” exclaimed, “What's this? Is there someone buried here?” (It was Pardner's Monument that she had removed from the Dallas Cemetery!) My ears were perked up and waiting to hear Pardner's reply. “Oh, dahlin', folks are buried all over these old hills. There's no tellin' where or who all. Just keep working around it.” Pardner didn't dare look through the window at me, knowing that I heard and would be laughing. I couldn't wait to tell Spike and her grandsons!

At the Kamp Cemetery, there were several Labrador dogs buried that had belonged to Joe, Jamie Jo and Spike. There was also one horse, “Old Paint,” from in the '30's. The only person buried there at that time was “Uncle Bob” Calden, 100 years old. Pardner confided in “Red” Smith, a maintenance man, “Red, when I die, I know Darnell will be upset, so; I want you to make sure that I am not buried on top of that horse.”

Pardner never missed a day of driving her boat across the lake, and climbing the steps to the top of the hill to nourish the flowers, plants, and Kampers until she was 93 years of age, then Spike drove her to Kamp. Joe often took her fishing until her last days (she was still teaching him how to catch fish.) Pardner lived a five weeks longer than 100 years.

Her monument was moved from my office yard to
the Kamp Cemetery:
“Monnie Hays Hackney
1894 – 1994”

A bronze plaque reads:
“Pardner
Kamps' Flower Lady
Love in Bloom”
Note: She was not buried on top of “Old Paint.”

Passing The Baton

Spike enthusiastically stepped down in 1979 to make Joe the President of Kanakuk Kamps. Joe exhibited the tremendous talent of leadership and was loyal to Kanakuk's responsibility to youth and its development. He never missed a summer at Kanakuk even though we urged him, as a teenager, to take a summer to travel. He had been a Counselor since the year after he was Chief of the Cherokees, and later a Director of K-2.

> "You plan them; I'll build them; they'll come."

When Joe became President in 1979, Spike was 65 years of age. He then formally retired with the intent of giving Joe support, counsel (when requested) and supervision. He also would build the new Kamps Joe yearned to establish. When K-2 for teenagers was just a dream and desire in Joe's heart, Joe and Spike collaborated and planned to continue as land and means indicated. "You plan them; I'll build them; they'll come."

Spike and Joe made a marvelous and bonding friendship. They were a great same-minded same-end results-team. Joe had a vision for Kamps of different age-groups and types and Spike had the expertise and ingenuity to get the job done.

As soon as Joe selected the land, Spike went to work! He had mentally planned out the fields and sites for the Sports activities at K-2. Spike first cleared the grounds of trees and shrubs in order to seed the playing fields. Thick green turf needed lots of time to be fertilized and age for safe athletic events. Spike had a little trailer/office set upon the premises. He drove home about two or three times a week.

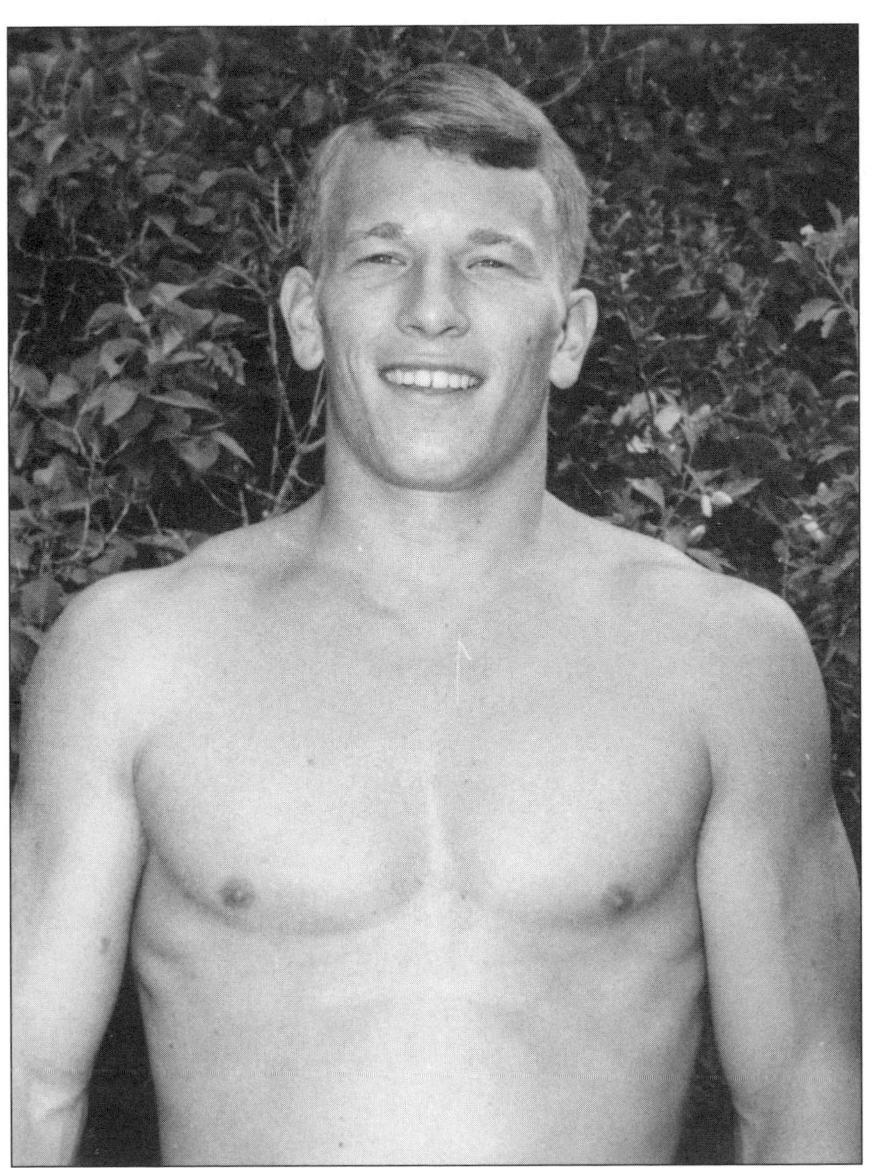

In the meantime, after K-2 was in full operation a few years, Joe, after the closing for the summer, opened the Kamp to inner-city groups from St. Louis and Kansas City. That gave him a vision to build beautiful inner-city Kamps from Cities and States for all summer to run the full summer long. From this KAA was born and was set up as a Non-Profit Organization. It had its own President and Board, independent of Kanakuk Kamps.

KAA has expanded under their own government and has expanded from the first and second Kamps that Spike supervised and built to two newer ones. A Payne Stewart Course in his honor was dedicated the year of 2006. (Payne Stewart's daughter and son were Kampers at KANAKUK KAMPS before and after he was killed.)

"... and Jesus grew in stature, ..."

"... and Jesus grew in stature, in wisdom, and
in favor with God and man." – Luke 2:52

Growing is a wonderful quality to be respected in youth, and Kanakuk Kamps through all the years have grown by this scripture. Many Kamp Talks on this scripture have been presented at the Kamp Churches, and each speaker has had a different approach and all have been meaningful and thought-provoking. "Precious things come in small packages." Luke's fourteen words alone stand tall giving a splendid message how to "grow."

When Spike and I purchased Kamp Kanakuk, our goal was to build on its already staunch and sterling foundation to bring more Kampers each summer.

Three years later the 60 boys' enrollment had increased to 85 – 90 - 120, then 160 and climbing. This was not because of any of the physical alterations such as rebuilding cabins, or athletic fields, but predominantly because of Coach Bill Lantz's philosophies and goals that remain the important basis of Kanakuks successes today. Spike hustled and pursued the endeavor to enlarge the enrollment and opened the girls' Kanakomo Kamp.

Over and over again down through the years, parents have asked, "When are you going to build a Kamp for parents?" At the end of Kamp, seeing their children vibrant and enthusiastic around their counselors and cabin friends, the parents feel a yearning to experience the same carefree and jubilant stress-free outing, as a Dad and Mom – a family that plays and prays together.

Through Joe's and Debbie Jo's dedication and devotion, a Family Kamp, K-Kauai, has answered the question asked for so many years. The first summer of 2006 has received accolades, and registration for its second year looks great.

"Growing" (maturing) can be wonderful when there is a Christian-worthy purpose and development for others. Today, Kanakuk keeps growing in stature, wisdom, and favor with God and man. The Luke 2:52 Messages, the Four Square Life, and The I'm Third Talks are the outstanding and bottom-line foundation for Kanakuk's stability and perspective through the past 81 years. Joe and Debbie Jo have grown in His wisdom and His favor, and their love and dedication to Youth abound through His Amazing Grace.